THE PREACHER'S PORTRAIT

By the same author: —

BASIC CHRISTIANITY
WHAT CHRIST THINKS OF THE CHURCH
FUNDAMENTALISM AND EVANGELISM
MEN WITH A MESSAGE
YOUR CONFIRMATION

The Preacher's Portrait

Some New Testament Word Studies

by John R. W. Stott

Rector of All Souls
Langham Place, London

nans Publishing Company
l Rapids, Michigan

Library of Congress catalog card number 61-17392.

ISBN 0-8028-1191-4

Reprinted, October 1984

Biblical quotations are from the Revised Standard Version
'ise stated.

THE PAYTON LECTURES

The present volume is an expansion of the ninth series of Payton Lectures delivered by the Reverend John R. W. Stott April 10-14, 1961, at Fuller Theological Seminary, Pasadena, California.

The Payton Lectureship was instituted in memory of Dr. and Mrs. John E. Payton, the parents of Mrs. Charles E. Fuller, wife of the founder of Fuller Theological Seminary. The bequest provides for an annual series of lectures by a competent scholar. The lectures must fall within these areas: the uniqueness or confirmation of the historic Christian faith, the confutation of non-Christian or sub-Christian views, or the formulation of Biblical doctrines.

PREFACE

In this book I am not directly concerned with preaching "techniques," with what the late Dr. W. E. Sangster of Westminster Central Hall has called, "The Craft of the Sermon," its construction and illustration, nor am I directly concerned with the problems of "communication." I do not doubt that there are methods of preaching which need to be learned, nor that communication is a vitally important subject in our day, when the gulf between the church and the secular world is already so disastrously wide that few bridges are left by which the two remain in contact.

I am concerned, I submit, with even more basic things. I propose that we should take a fresh look at some of the words employed in the New Testament to describe the preacher and his task. We need, I believe, to gain in the Church today a clearer view of God's revealed ideal for the preacher, what he is and how he is to do his work. So I shall be considering his message and his authority, the character of the proclamation he is called to make, the vital necessity of his own experience of the Gospel, the nature of his motive, the source of his power, and the moral qualities which should characterize him, notably humility, gentleness and love. This, I suggest, is *the preacher's portrait*, a portrait painted by the hand of God Himself on the broad canvas of the New Testament.

I am hesitant to write on this subject at all. I do not pose as an expert; I am far from it. I have only begun myself to learn the rudiments of preaching. But as God in His grace has called me to the ministry of the Word, I am deeply anxious to conform my ministry to the perfect pattern He has given us in the same Word.   —J. R. W. S.

CONTENTS

CHAPTER ONE

A STEWARD

The Preacher's Message and Authority

THE first important question which confronts the preacher is: 'What shall I say, and whence shall I derive my message?' Several wrong answers have been given to this fundamental question regarding the origin and content of the preacher's message, and I must begin with these, negatively.

Not a Prophet

First, the Christian preacher is not a prophet. That is, he does not derive his message from God as a direct and original revelation. Of course, the word 'prophet' is used loosely by some people today. It is not uncommon to hear a man who preaches with passion described as possessing prophetic fire; and a preacher who can discern the signs of the times, who sees the hand of God in the history of the day and seeks to interpret the significance of political and social trends, is sometimes said to be a prophet and to have prophetic insight. But I suggest that this kind of use of the title 'prophet' is an improper one.

What, then, is a prophet? The Old Testament regarded him as the immediate mouthpiece of God. When God appointed Aaron to speak the words of Moses to Pharaoh, He explained this arrangement to Moses in these words: 'See, I make you as God to Pharaoh, and Aaron your brother shall be your prophet'. And again, 'You shall speak to him [Aaron] and put the words in his mouth; and I will be with your mouth and with his mouth, and will teach you what you shall do. He shall speak for you to the people; and he shall be a mouth

for you, and you shall be to him as God' (Ex. 7:1, 2, 4:10-17).
This makes it plain that the prophet was God's 'mouth',
through whom God spoke His words to man. Similarly, in
describing the prophet like Moses who should arise, God
said: 'I will put my words in his mouth, and he shall speak
to them all that I command him. . . . He shall speak in my
Name' (Dt. 18:18, 19). The prophet spoke neither his own
words nor in his own name, but God's words and in God's
Name. It is this conviction that God had spoken to them and
revealed His secrets to them (Amos 3:7, 8) which accounts
for the familiar prophetic formulae such as 'the word of the
Lord came unto . . .', 'Thus says the Lord', 'Hear the word
of the Lord', and 'the mouth of the Lord has spoken it'.

The essential characteristic of the prophet was neither that
he foretold the future, nor that he interpreted the present,
activity of God, but that he spoke God's word. As Peter
put it, 'No prophecy [that is no true prophecy, as opposed to
the lies of the false prophets whom he goes on to describe]
ever came by the impulse of man, but men moved by the
Holy Spirit spoke from God' (2 Pet. 1:21).

The Christian preacher, therefore, is not a prophet. No
original revelation is given to him; his task is to expound
the revelation which has been given once for all. And however truly he preaches in the power of the Holy Spirit, he
is not 'inspired' by the Spirit in the sense in which the
prophets were. It is true that 'whoever speaks' is instructed
to do so 'as one who utters oracles of God' (1 Pet. 4:11).
This, however, is not because he is himself, or has received, a
fresh divine oracle, but because he is a steward (1 Pet. 4:10),
as we shall see later, to whom have been entrusted the Holy
Scriptures, which are 'the oracles of God' (Rom. 3:2). The
last occurrence in the Bible of the formula 'the word of God
came unto' refers to John the Baptist (Lk. 3:2). He was a
true prophet. There were also prophets in New Testament
days like Agabus (Acts 21:10), and prophecy is mentioned
as a spiritual gift (Rom. 12:6; 1 Cor. 12:10, 29; Eph. 4:11),

but this gift is no longer bestowed upon men in the Church. Now that the written word of God is available to us all, the word of God in prophetic utterance is no longer needed. The word of God does not come to men today. It has come once and for all; men must now come to it.

Not an Apostle

Secondly, the Christian preacher is not an apostle. Of course the Church is 'apostolic', both in being built on the foundation of apostolic doctrine and in being sent into the world to preach the gospel. But missionary church-builders should not properly be called 'apostles'. It is incorrect to speak of 'Hudson Taylor, apostle of China', or 'Judson, apostle of Burma', as you would speak of 'Paul, apostle of the Gentiles'. Recent study has confirmed that the apostles were unique. Karl Heinrich Rengstorf in his article on 'Apostleship' in Gerhard Kittel's famous *Theologisches Wöterbuch*[1] argues that the apostles of Jesus were equivalent to the Jewish *shaliachim* who were special messengers sent to the dispersion with full authority to teach, so that, they said, 'the one sent by a person is as this person himself'. Rengstorf writes: '. . . whereas the other verbs connote a sending as such, *apostellein* carries with it the ideas of special purpose, mission or commission, authorization and responsibility'.[2] *Apostolos*, he says, is 'always the designation of a man who is sent as ambassador, and indeed, an authorized ambassador. The Greek word *apostolos* merely provides the form; the content and idea come to light from the *shaliach* of Rabbinic Judaism'.[3]

Norval Geldenhuys, in his valuable book *Supreme Authority*, carries Rengstorf's article to its logical conclusion. The New Testament apostle is 'one chosen and sent with a

---

1. Karl Heinrich Rengstorf, *Theologisches Wörterbuch zum Neuen Testament* (1932/3), article 'Apostleship,' translated by J. R. Coates (London: A. & C. Black, 1952).
2. *Ibid.*, Introduction, p. xii.
3. *Ibid.*, p. 26.

special commission as the fully authorized representative of the sender'.[4] In naming the twelve chosen disciples 'apostles' Jesus indicated that they were to be 'His delegates whom He would send with the commission to teach and to act in His Name and on His authority'.[5] He gave them a special authority (e.g., Lk. 9:1, 2, 10), which they later claimed to possess and exercised. Paul maintained that he was an apostle too, on a par with the twelve, by direct appointment of the Risen Jesus. 'A personal commission was the only ground of apostleship',[6] to which should be added an encounter with Jesus after the resurrection. Geldenhuys's conclusion is: 'Never again could or can there be persons who possess all these qualifications to be the *shaliachim* of Jesus'.[7] Even Rengstorf, who says 'we do not know how many apostles there were in the early days, but they must have been fairly numerous',[8] adds that the apostolate 'was limited to the first generation and did not become an ecclesiastical office'. Again, 'every apostle is a disciple, but not every disciple is an apostle'.[9] Geldenhuys quotes from Alfred Plummer's article on 'Apostle' in Hastings' *Dictionary of the Apostolic Church*: 'No Transmission of so exceptional an office was possible'.[10]

This evidence suggests a close parallel between the Old Testament prophets and the New Testament apostles, to which Rengstorf draws attention. 'The linking of the apostle's consciousness with that of the prophet . . . emphasizes absolutely the fact that what he preaches is revelation, and guards against every kind of human corruption.' 'Like the prophet, Paul is the servant of his message.'[11] 'The parallel

---

4. Norval Geldenhuys, *Supreme Authority* (Grand Rapids: Eerdmans, 1953), pp. 53, 54.
5. *Ibid.*, p. 54.
6. Rengstorf, *op. cit.*, p. 43.
7. Geldenhuys, *op. cit.*, p. 74.
8. Rengstorf, *op. cit.*, p. 44.
9. *Ibid.*, p. 33.
10. Geldenbuys, *op. cit.*, p. 74.
11. Rengstorf, *op. cit.*, p. 59.

between the apostles and prophets is justified, because they are both bearers of revelation.'[12]

Thus, as the word 'prophet' should be reserved for those men in both Old and New Testaments to whom the word of God came direct, whether their message has survived or not, so the designation 'apostle' must be reserved for the Twelve and Paul, who were specially commissioned and invested with authority by Jesus as His *shaliachim*. These men were unique. They have no successors.

Not a False Prophet or Apostle

Thirdly, the Christian preacher is (or should be) neither a false prophet nor a false apostle.[13] We read of both in Scripture, and the difference between the true and the spurious is most clearly defined in Jeremiah 23. The true prophet was one who 'has stood in the council of the Lord to perceive and hear His word'. He has 'given heed to His word and listened' (vv. 18, 22). False prophets, on the other hand, spoke 'visions of their own minds, not from the mouth of the Lord' (v. 16). They prophesied 'the deceit of their own heart' (v. 26). They told lies in the name of God (v. 25). The contrast is vividly made in verse 28: 'Let the prophet who has a dream tell the dream, but let him who has my word speak my word faithfully. What has straw in common with wheat? says the Lord'. Again, those who heard the message of prophets were listening either to 'every man's own word' or to 'the words of the living God' (v. 36).

Although there are, strictly speaking, no prophets or apostles today, I fear there are false prophets and false apostles. They speak their own words instead of God's Word. Their message originates in their own mind. These are men who like to ventilate their own opinions on religion, ethics, theology

12. Rengstorf, *op. cit.*, p. 60. Cf. Eph. 2:20, 3:5.
13. The expression' false apostle' occurs in 2 Cor. 11:13 only, although cf. Rev. 2:2. 'Paul means by it one who gives himself out as an apostle of Christ without having his authorization' (Rengstorf, *op. cit.*, p. 67).

or politics. They may be conventional enough to introduce their sermon with a scripture text, but the text bears little or no relation to the sermon which follows, nor is any attempt made to interpret the text in its context. It has been truly said that such a text without a context is a pretext. Very often also, these preachers, like the false prophets of the Old Testament, speak smooth words, saying 'Peace, peace' when there is no peace (Jer. 6:14, 8:11, cf. 23:17), and they withhold the less flattering aspects of the gospel in order not to offend popular taste (cf. Jer. 5:30, 31).

Not a 'Babbler'

Fourthly, the Christian preacher is not a 'babbler'. This is the word which the Athenian philosophers used on the Areopagus to describe Paul. 'What would this babbler say?' they asked with scorn (Acts 17:18). The Greek word is *spermologos*, which means a 'seed-picker'. It was used in its literal sense of seed-eating birds, and especially, I believe, by Aristophanes and Aristotle of the rook. Metaphorically, it came to be applied to a scavenger, a 'guttersnipe',[14] 'one who makes his living by picking up scraps, a ragpicker'.[15] From this it was transferred to the gossip or chatterbox, 'one who picks up and retails scraps of knowledge'.[16] The 'babbler' trades in ideas like second-hand merchandise, picking up bits and pieces wherever he finds them. His sermons are a veritable ragbag.

Now it is clearly not wrong in a sermon to quote from somebody else's words or writings. Indeed, the wise preacher keeps a book or file of memorable and illuminating quotations; and, provided that they are used judiciously and honestly, with due acknowledgement, they can add light, weight and point to a subject. If I may immediately practise what I

14. Liddell & Scott, *A Greek-English Lexicon,* rev. ed. (Oxford: Clarendon Press, 1925-40).
15. W. F. Arndt & F. W. Gingrich, *A Greek-English Lexicon of the New Testament and other early Christian Literature* (Cambridge: Cambridge University Press, 1957).
16. Liddell & Scott, *op. cit.*

preach and quote from someone else, although I cannot acknowledge the witticism because I do not know who first made it: 'If you borrow from one man they call it "plagiarism"; if you borrow from a thousand, they call it "research" '!

But careful quoting from other sources is not necessarily 'babbling'. The essential characteristic of the babbler is that he has no mind of his own. His present opinion is that of the last person with whom he spoke. He relays other men's ideas without sifting them, or weighing them, or making them his own. Like the false prophets whom Jeremiah castigated, he uses his 'tongue' only, but not his mind or heart, and is guilty of 'stealing' his message from others (Jer. 23:30, 31).

A Steward

What, then, is the preacher? He is a steward. 'This is how one should regard us, as servants of Christ and stewards of the mysteries of God. Moreover, it is required of stewards that they be found trustworthy' (1 Cor. 4:1, 2). The steward is the trustee and dispenser of another person's goods. So the preacher is a steward of God's mysteries, that is, of the self-revelation which God has entrusted to men and which is now preserved in the Scriptures. The Christian preacher's message, therefore, is derived not directly from the mouth of God, as if he were a prophet or apostle, nor from his own mind, like the false prophets, nor undigested from the minds and mouths of other men, like the babbler, but from the once revealed and now recorded Word of God, of which he is a privileged steward.

The concept of the household steward was more familiar in the ancient world than the modern. Nowadays, Christian people associate the word 'stewardship' with campaigns to raise money, and in our everyday vocabulary a 'steward' belongs only to ocean-going liners and big residential institutions. But in Bible times every well-to-do householder had a steward to manage his household affairs, his property, his farm or vineyard, his accounts and his slaves. We meet

the steward several times in the Old Testament.[17] No single
Hebrew word is used to identify him, but his office is
recognisable in several words, and he is found particularly in
the noble families and royal courts of Judah, Egypt and Babylon. Thus Joseph had a steward in Egypt. This 'steward of
his house' (R.S.V.) was charged with the care of Joseph's
guests. He saw that they had water for their feet and fodder
for their donkeys. He was responsible for the slaughter of
animals for the table and for the preparation of meals. He
seems also to have supplied food to those who came to buy it,
and he received money in payment. He had slaves under him
(Gen. 43:16:25, 44:1-13). Similarly, the kings of Judah had a
steward in charge of the royal household.[18] During the
reign of King Hezekiah the steward was named Shebna (Is.
22:15 [R.S.V.]).[19] He seems to have been an ambitious
man and to have enriched himself with 'splendid chariots', perhaps at the expense of the household account. But God tells
Shebna that he is to be deposed and replaced by Eliakim, the
son of Hilkiah: 'I will clothe him with your robe, and will
bind your girdle on him, and will commit your authority to
his hand; and he shall be a father to the inhabitants of
Jerusalem and to the house of Judah. And I will place on
his shoulder the key of the house of David. . .' (Is. 22:21, 22).
From this it is evident that the steward was a man of authority
in the household, exercising a fatherly supervision over its
members, and that the symbol of his office was a key, no
doubt to the stores.[20]

In King Nebuchadnezzar's court at Babylon, the chief of
the eunuchs put Daniel and his three companions in the care

17. Cf. Gen. 15:2. It may have been Eliezer who was entrusted with
the task of finding a wife for Isaac (Gen. 24).

18. David had officials who are described in 1 Chron. 28:1 as 'the
stewards of all the property and cattle of the king and his sons'. One
of Solomon's 'high officials' was Ahishar, who 'was in charge of the
palace' (1 Ki. 4:6).

19. The A. V. has 'treasurer'.

20. He is described in 2 Ki. 18, 19 and Is. 36, 37 (R.S.V.) as being 'over
the household'.

of someone whom the A.V. calls 'Melzar'. The word probably indicates an office rather than a proper name, an 'overseer', and the R.S.V. renders it 'steward'. It was his task to train men for palace service, issuing them daily rations and using his discretion whether these were the rich food and wine of the court or the simple vegetables for which Daniel asked (Dn. 1:8-6).

These Old Testament examples are paralleled in the New. Herod Antipas had a steward at court, a man called Chuza, whose wife, Joanna, was a disciple of Jesus and helped to provide for Him from her means (Lk. 8:3). Again, the scene in several of our Lord's parables is set in some great household, in which the steward occupies a position of responsibility. In the Parable of the Labourers in the Vineyard, the steward is ordered by the householder, the owner of the vineyard, to pay the labourers their wages (Mt. 20:1, 8), while the Unjust Steward was employed by 'a rich man', whose goods he was accused of 'wasting'. He was evidently a very responsible person, ordering the provisions and paying the bills, for he was able to falsify the accounts by reducing the liabilities of his master's debtors and apparently to escape detection in the process (Lk. 16:1-9).

We are now in a position to reconstruct the situation in a wealthy household in Bible times. We can do so by considering the group of words cognate with the verb *oikeō*, dwell. There are five important ones. First, there is *oikia* or *oikos*, the house itself.[21] Secondly, there is *oikeioi*, the household. Its only secular use in the New Testament is 1 Timothy 5:8, where the apostle says that if anybody makes no provision 'for his relatives, and especially for his own family' (*oikeiōn*), he is 'worse than an unbeliever'.[22] Thirdly, comes the word

---

21. *Oikia* was, strictly, the whole house and *oikos* an apartment within it, but both words were used for a house or building in which people dwelt.

22. The similar word *oikiakos* occurs only in Mt. 10:25, 36; and both *oikos* and *oikia* were used of the residents as well as the building, of the household as well as the house (e.g., *oikos* in Acts 7:10, 10:2 and *oikia* in John 4:53 and Phil. 4:22).

oikodespotēs, the householder, the master of the house, called
in the A.V. 'the goodman of the house' (e.g., Mk. 14:14).[23]
He rules or manages the household, and the verb indicating
his work (*oikodespoteō*) occurs in 1 Timothy 5:14. Fourthly,
there is *oiketēs*, the house servant, or, as he is called in Africa,
'the house boy'. *Doulos* was the general word for a slave,
but *oiketēs* particularly described the servant who worked
in the house. The Latin equivalent is *domesticus*, which originally included all who lived under the same roof or in the
same *domus*, but later came to mean the servant or,
as we might say, 'domestic'.[24]

Fifthly, there is *oikonomos*, the housekeeper or steward,
whose office is termed *oikonomia*, stewardship.[25] These words
come from *oikos*, a house, and *nemō*, dispense or manage, and
from them, of course, are derived our words economy, econo-
mic(s), and economical. The definition of *oikonomos* given
in the lexicon of Grimm & Thayer is worth quoting in full:
'The manager of a household or of household affairs; especially a steward, manager, superintendent . . . to whom the head
of a house or proprietor has entrusted the management of
his affairs, the care of receipts and expenditures, and the duty
of dealing out the proper portion to every servant and even
to the children not yet of age.'[26] Whether he was a free
man or a slave, he occupied a responsible position between the

23. In Mt. 10:25 the householder and the household are clearly
distinguished.
24. *Oiketes* is found four times in the N. T. (Lk. 16:13, Acts 10:7,
Rom. 14:4 and 1 Pet. 2:18). Cf. *oiketeia* in Mt. 24:45 as a collective
noun for servants or 'staff'.
25. The nouns *oikonomos,* steward, and *oikonomia,* stewardship, are
found together with the verb *oikonomein,* to act as steward, in the
Parable of the Unjust Steward (Lk. 16:1-9). In later Greek the verb
developed a very general meaning, signifying simply to 'make arrangements' (Moulton & Milligan, *The Vocabulary of the Greek Testament,*
p. 443 [Grand Rapids: Eerdmans]), to transact any business, to administer or manage anything.
26. *A Greek-English Lexicon of the New Testament,* 2nd ed. rev.
(Edinburgh: T. & T. Clark, 1892), pp. 440-41.

householder and his household.[27]   The word is even used
in Romans 16:23 of Erastus, who appears to have been 'the
city treasurer' (R.S.V.) of Corinth.   In Galatians 4:2 a child
is said to be under both *epitropoi* and *oikonomoi*, the former
being his legal guardians and his teachers, while the latter
will have taken care of his property during his minority.

Put together, these five words describe the social situation
in a wealthy family.   The *oikos* (house) was inhabited by the
oikeioi (household), consisting of both children and slaves.
The head of the house was the *oikodespotēs* (householder),
who had both a number of *oiketai* (household servants) under
him and also an *oikonomos* (housekeeper or steward) to
supervise them, to feed the household, and to administer the
affairs and accounts of the house and estate.

It is not surprising that the early believers saw in this
social pattern a picture of the Christian Church.   Their
distinctive name for God was 'Father', and since a father was
normally a householder, it was natural to think of the Christian family as being God's 'household'.   The picture cannot
be pressed in detail, however.   Nor is the New Testament
usage entirely consistent, for, although God is always the
householder, the Church is now the house in which He
dwells,[28] now His household, which is a 'household of faith',[29]
and now His house servants who are responsible to Him for
their work (Rom. 14:4).

All Christian people are also God's stewards, who have been
entrusted with certain 'goods', not for their own benefit but
for the blessing of the household at large.   The Parables of
the Talents and of the Pounds illustrate the Christian's responsibility to improve and use the opportunities and gifts which

27. The Unjust Steward seems to have been a free man (Lk. 16:1-9).
The stewards in Mt. 24:45 and Lk. 12:42, 43 are distinctly called
slaves.

28. The tabernacle was God's *oikos* (Mk. 2:26).   So was the temple
(Mk. 11:17).   But His Church is now His temple (1 Cor. 3:16, 6:19;
Eph. 2:21, 22), cf. Heb. 10:21.

29. *Oikos* in 1 Tim. 3:15, 1 Pet. 4:17 (cf. Heb. 3:2-6), and *oikeios* in
Gal. 6:10, Eph. 2:19.

Christ has given him (Mt. 25:14-30, Lk. 19:12-28). The steward must neither hoard nor waste his master's goods committed to his trust. He must dispense them to the household. As Christians we are all, in Peter's memorable phrase, 'stewards of God's varied (literally, 'variegated', or 'many coloured') grace' (1 Pet. 4:10), and he makes it plain that 'each' is to use his gifts 'for one another'. He goes on to give two examples, speaking and rendering service, and it is the former which is of particular concern to us.

The Christian ministry is a sacred stewardship. The presbyter-bishop was described by Paul as 'God's steward' (Tit. 1:7). Paul regarded himself and Apollos as 'stewards of the mysteries of God' (1 Cor. 4:1) and, although Paul was steward of a special 'mystery' which had been personally revealed to him, (Eph. 3:1-3, 7-9) this is not a designation for apostles only, since he applies it to Apollos as well as to himself, and Apollos was not an apostle like Paul. 'Steward' is a descriptive title for all who have the privilege of preaching God's word, particularly in the ministry. As we shall see in Chapter 5, the Corinthians were showing an exaggerated deference to their leaders. Paul rebukes their hero worship. '*This* is how one should regard us', he says, 'we are merely Christ's underlings and the stewards of Another's goods.' Such is the subordinate position which we occupy. The 'goods' of which the Christian preacher is a steward are termed 'the mysteries of God'. *Musterion* in the New Testament is not a dark, unexplained enigma, but a truth which has been made known, which can only be known because God has disclosed it, which has been hitherto concealed but is now revealed, and into which God has initiated men. So 'the mysteries of God' are God's open secrets, the sum total of His self-revelation which is now embodied in the Scriptures.[30] Of these revealed 'mysteries' the Christian preacher is the steward, charged to make them further known to the household.

30. Cf. Christ's use of the word in connection with the Kingdom of God (Mt. 13:2).

From this great stewardship metaphor, the Christian preacher may learn four important lessons, which are different aspects of the 'faithfulness' required of stewards.

The Preacher's Incentive and Message

The first truth concerns *the source of the preacher's incentive.* Preaching is hard work. The preacher is often tempted to become dispirited. He needs powerful incentives to strengthen his flagging soul, and there is no doubt that he can find one here. St. Paul certainly did. He was a steward of God's mysteries, 'a trustee of the secrets of God' (1 Cor. 4:1, Phillips). The gospel was a sacred trust committed to him. Several times in his epistles he writes in these terms.[31] This trust weighed heavily upon him. 'I am entrusted with a commission', he said, and the word he used here is again *oikonomia*, stewardship (1 Cor. 9:17). Again, 'Necessity is laid upon me. Woe to me if I do not preach the gospel!' and 'I am under obligation' to preach the gospel (1 Cor. 9:16; Rom. 1:14). 'It is required of stewards', he wrote 'that they be found trustworthy'. The steward has received a trust; he must show himself worthy of this trust. The householder depends on him. The household are looking to him for provisions. He must not fail.

Secondly, the stewardship metaphor indicates *the content of the preacher's message.* Indeed, if the metaphor teaches anything, it teaches that the preacher does not supply his own message; he is supplied with it. If the steward is not expected to feed the household out of his own pocket, the preacher is not to provide his own message by his own ingenuity. Many New Testament metaphors indicate that same truth, that the preacher's task is to proclaim a message which has been given to him. The preacher is a sower of seed, and 'the seed is the word of God' (Lk. 8:11). He is a herald, and he is told what good news he is to proclaim. He takes part in the

31. E.g., 1 Thess. 2:4 and his references in the Epistles to Timothy to 'the deposit'.

building of an edifice, and both the foundation and the materials are provided (e.g., 1 Cor. 3:10-15).[32] Similarly, he is the steward of goods which are committed to him by the householder.

This is the second way in which the steward is required to be faithful, namely, to the goods themselves. He is to guard them from harm and to be diligent in dispensing them to the household. The Apostle lays great emphasis in writing to Timothy on his responsibility to 'guard the deposit'. The precious gospel had been committed to his faithful care. It was a 'good deposit'. He must stand guard over it, as sentinels over a city or warders in a gaol (1 Tim. 1:11, 6:20, 2 Tim. 1:12, 14 (R.S.V.).[33] If we are good stewards, we shall not presume to 'tamper with God's word' (2 Cor. 4:2), nor to 'corrupt' it (2 Cor. 2:17 [A.V.]). Our task is 'the open statement of the truth' (2 Cor. 4:2; cf. Acts 4:29, 31; Phil. 1:14; 2 Tim. 4:2; Heb. 13:7). This, so far as it goes, is a good definition of preaching. Preaching is a 'manifestation', *phanerōsis*, of the truth which stands written in the Scriptures. Therefore, every sermon should be, in some sense, an expository sermon. The preacher may use illustrations from political, ethical, and social fields to illumine and enforce the Biblical principles he is seeking to unfold, but the pulpit is no place for purely political commentary, ethical exhortation or social debate. We are to preach 'the word of God', and nothing else (Col. 1:25).

Moreover, we are called to preach the whole range of the Word of God. This was the Apostle Paul's ambition. He recognized that his 'divine stewardship' was 'to make the word of God fully known', that is, to preach it fully and completely. Indeed, he could claim, in the presence of the Ephesian elders: 'I did not shrink from declaring to you the whole counsel of God' (Acts 20:27). How few preachers could

---

32. According to v. 11 the foundation to be laid is already lying there.
33. 1 Tim. 1:4, where human speculations are contrasted with 'the divine stewardship'.

advance the same claim! Most of us ride a few of our favourite hobby-horses to death. We pick and choose from the Scriptures, selecting doctrines we like and passing over those we dislike or find difficult. In this way we are guilty of withholding from the household some of the provision which the Divine Householder in His wise bounty has supplied for them. Some not only subtract from, but add to, the Scripture, while others presume to contradict what stands written in God's Word.

Let me use a homely illustration. The Englishman's favourite breakfast dish is eggs and bacon. We will suppose that a certain householder issued his steward or housekeeper eggs and bacon, with instructions to dispense them to the household for breakfast on four successive mornings. On Monday morning the steward threw them into the garbage can and gave them fish instead. That is contradiction, and his master was angry. On Tuesday morning he gave them eggs only, but not bacon. That is subtraction, and his master was again angry. On Wednesday morning he gave them eggs and bacon and sausages. That is addition, and his master was still angry. But in the end, on Thursday morning, he gave them eggs and bacon — nothing else, nothing less, nothing more, and his master was well pleased with him at last!

The household of God urgently needs faithful stewards who will dispense to it systematically the whole Word of God, not the New Testament only but the Old as well, not the best known texts only, but also the less known, not just the passages which favour the preacher's particular prejudices, but those which do not! We need more men today of the calibre of Charles Simeon of Cambridge, who wrote in his preface to the *Horae Homileticae*: 'The author is no friend to systematizers in theology. He has endeavoured to derive from the Scriptures alone *his* views of religion, and to them it is his wish to adhere with scrupulous fidelity; never wresting any portion of the Word of God to favour a particular opinion, but giving to every part of it that sense, which it seems to him to have been designed by its great Author to convey'.[34]   Consequently, he was 'free from all the trammels of human systems', could 'pronounce every part of God's blessed Word, *ore rotundo,* mincing nothing, fearing nothing', and did not consider whose particular system it might be thought to support.[35]   Only such faithful exposition of the whole Word of God will deliver us and our congregations from little whims and fancies (whether ours or theirs), and from a more serious fanaticism and extravagance.   Only so, too, shall we teach them to discern between what has been clearly revealed and what has not, as we do not fear to be dogmatic about the former but are content to remain agnostic about the latter (see Dt. 29:29).

Besides, the Church needs an instructed laity, who will not be like 'children tossed to and fro and carried about with every wind of doctrine' (Eph. 4:14), but who are growing in their knowledge of God and of His Word, and who are thereby able to resist the subtle encroachment of modern cults.   Nothing can bring about this happy state of affairs but the solid, systematic, didactic preaching of the whole Word of God.

Such conscientious teaching is not possible without careful planning months in advance.   We shall need to examine the scope of our sermons to see if there are whole areas of truth which we have been avoiding and others on which we may have been concentrating too much.   One way to escape extremes of neglect and overemphasis is to work steadily through books of the Bible or at least whole chapters, expounding everything, shirking nothing.   Another way is to plan regular or occasional courses of sermons, giving a balanced and comprehensive treatment of some aspects of revealed truth.   And do not let us be fainthearted and imagine the

34. London: Richard Watts (1819), pp. 4, 5.
35. Simeon, Letter to Thomason, 1822.

laity could not endure such things! Remember the wise words of Richard Baxter to the people of Kidderminster: "Were you but as willing to get the knowledge of God and heavenly things as you are to know how to work in your trade, you would have set yourself to it before this day, and you would have spared no cost or pains till you had got it. But you account seven years little enough to learn your trade and will not bestow one day in seven in diligent learning the matters of your salvation'.

However, in recommending that the preacher should aim to expound the whole Word of God, I do not mean that he should be clumsy or unimaginative about it. The same Paul who said he had not shrunk from 'declaring . . . the whole counsel of God' also said, and in the same speech, 'I did not shrink from declaring to you anything that was profitable' (Acts 20:20, 27). Of course 'all Scripture is . . . profitable' (2 Tim. 3:16), but all is not equally profitable for the same people at the same time. The wise steward varies the diet which he gives to the household. He studies their needs and uses his discretion in supplying them with suitable food. The steward has no say in determining what goes into the larder; it is stocked for him by the householder. But it is his responsibility to decide what comes out of it, and when, and in what measure. This is another aspect of the steward's faithfulness, this time not to the householder or the goods, but to the household. As Jesus said, 'Who then is the faithful and wise steward, whom his master will set over his household, to give them their portion of food at the proper time?' (Lk. 12:42). The steward's wisdom and faithfulness will be displayed in the balance and suitability of the diet which he gives the household. He must feed the family from the stores with which he has been issued, but, since he must prevail on them to eat what he supplies, he takes pains to make it palatable. He uses his imagination to render the food appetising. He even coaxes them to eat it, as a mother does her child. So the good steward will be as familiar with the needs and predilections of the household as he is with the contents of his store cupboard.

All this is of great importance. It is not enough for the preacher to know the Word of God; he must know the people to whom he proclaims it. He must not, of course, falsify God's Word in order to make it more appealing. He cannot dilute the strong medicine of Scripture to render it more sweet to the taste. But he may seek to present it to the people in such a way as to commend it to them. For one thing, he will make it simple. This surely is what Paul meant when he told Timothy to be 'a workman who has no need to be ashamed, rightly handling the word of truth' (2 Tim. 2:15). The verb, *orthotomounta*, means literally, 'cutting straight'. It was employed of road making and is, for instance, used in the LXX of Proverbs 3:6: 'He will make straight [A.V., "direct"] your paths'. Our exposition of the Scripture is to be so simple and direct, so easily intelligible, that it resembles a straight road. It is easy to follow it. It is like Isaiah's highway of the redeemed: even 'fools shall not err therein' (Is. 35:8). Such straight cutting of the Word of God is not easy. It requires much study, as we shall see later, not only of God's Word but of man's nature and of the world in which he lives. The expository preacher is a bridge builder, seeking to span the gulf between the Word of God and the mind of man. He must do his utmost to interpret the Scripture so accurately and plainly, and to apply it so forcefully, that the truth crosses the bridge.

The Preacher's Authority and Discipline

In the third place, the stewardship metaphor teaches us *the nature of the preacher's authority*. The preacher does have a certain authority. We should not be afraid or ashamed of it. Authority is not incompatible with humility. Professor James Stewart has written: 'It is quite mistaken to suppose that humility excludes conviction. G. K. Chesterton once penned some wise words about what he called "the dislocation of humility", — "What we suffer from today is humility in the wrong place. Modesty has moved from the organ of ambition. Modesty has settled upon the organ of conviction; where it was never meant to be. A man was meant to be doubtful about himself, but undoubting about the truth; this has been exactly reversed. We are on the road to producing a race of men too mentally modest to believe in the multiplication table." Humble and self-forgetting we must be always, but diffident and and apologetic about the gospel never'.[36]

But wherein does the preacher's authority lie? The preacher's authority is not that of the prophet. The Christian preacher cannot properly say 'Thus says the Lord', as did the prophets when introducing a direct message from God. He certainly dare not say 'Verily, verily I say unto you', as did the Son of God, speaking with the absolute authority of God, and as some dogmatic false prophets might, presuming to come in their own name. Nor should we become modern 'babblers' and say 'according to the best modern scholars', quoting some human authority, valuable as apt quotations may be in the right place. Instead, our formula, if we use one at all, should be the well-known, oft-repeated and quite proper phrase of Dr. Billy Graham, 'The Bible says'.

This is real authority. True, it is an indirect authority. It is not direct like that of the prophets, nor like that of the apostles, who issued commands and expected obedience (e.g., Paul in 2 Thess. 3), but it is still the authority of God. It is also true that the preacher who declares the Word with authority is under that Word and must submit to its authority himself. Although distinct from the congregation, he is one of them. Although he has the right to address them with direct 'I — you' speech, he will often prefer to use the first person plural 'we', because he is conscious that the Word he preaches applies

36. Stewart, *Heralds of God* (London: Hodder & Stoughton, 1946), p. 210.

to himself as much as to anyone else. Nevertheless, he can still speak with the authority of God.

Indeed, I am persuaded that the more the preacher has 'trembled' at God's Word himself (e.g., Ezra 9:4, 10:3; Is. 66:2, 5), and felt its authority upon his conscience and in his life, the more he will be able to preach it with authority to others. The stewardship metaphor does not convey the whole truth about the preacher and his authority. We are not to think of the preacher as an officious steward, nor as a Jewish scribe, giving dreary and scholastic interpretations of disputed points. True preaching is never stale or dull or academic, but fresh and pungent with the living authority of God. But the Scripture comes alive to the congregation only if it has come alive to the preacher first. Only if God has spoken to him through the Word which he preaches will they hear the voice of God through his lips.

Here, then, is the preacher's authority. It depends on the closeness of his adherence to the text he is handling, that is, on the accuracy with which he has understood it and on the forcefulness with which it has spoken to his own soul. In the ideal sermon it is the Word itself which speaks, or rather God in and through His Word. The less the preacher comes between the Word and its hearers, the better. What really feeds the household is the food which the householder supplies, not the steward who dispenses it. The Christian preacher is best satisfied when his person is eclipsed by the light which shines from the Scripture and when his voice is drowned by the Voice of God.

In the fourth place, the stewardship metaphor has a practical lesson to teach us about *the necessity of the preacher's discipline*. The faithful steward will make himself familiar with all the contents of his larder. The larder of Holy Scripture is so extensive, that even a life-time's arduous study will not fully disclose either its riches or its variety.

Expository preaching is a most exacting discipline. Perhaps that is why it is so rare. Only those will undertake it

who are prepared to follow the example of the apostles and
say, 'It is not right that we should give up preaching the
Word of God to serve tables. . . . We will devote ourselves
to prayer and to the ministry of the Word' (Acts 6:2, 4).
The systematic *preaching* of the Word is impossible without
the systematic *study* of it. It will not be enough to skim
through a few verses in daily Bible reading, nor to study a
passage only when we have to preach from it. No. We
must daily soak ourselves in the Scriptures. We must not just
study, as through a microscope, the linguistic minutiae of a few
verses, but take our telescope and scan the wide expanses
of God's Word, assimilating its grand theme of divine sover-
eignty in the redemption of mankind. 'It is blessed', wrote
C. H. Spurgeon, 'to eat into the very soul of the Bible until,
at last, you come to talk in scriptural language, and your
spirit is flavoured with the words of the Lord, so that your
blood is *Bibline* and the very essence of the Bible flows from
you.'[37]

Apart from this daily, dogged discipline of Bible study,
we shall need in particular to apply ourselves to the verse
or passage selected for exposition from the pulpit. We shall
need strength of mind to eschew short cuts. We must spend
time studying our text with painstaking thoroughness, medi-
tating on it, wrestling with it, worrying at it as a dog with
a bone, until it yields its meaning; and sometimes this process will be accompanied by toil and tears. We shall also
use all the resources of our library in this work — lexicon
and concordance, modern translations and commentaries.
But, above all, we must pray over the text, because the Holy
Spirit, who is the Book's ultimate author, is therefore its
best interpreter. 'Think over what I say', wrote Paul to
Timothy, 'for the Lord will grant you understanding in
everything' (2 Tim. 2:7). We must indeed do the thinking,
but it is God who gives the understanding. Even when the

37. Quoted in Richard Ellsworth Day, *The Shadow of the Broad
Brim* (Philadelphia: The Judson Press, 1934), p. 131.

text is understood, the preacher's work is only half done, for the elucidation of its meaning must be followed by its application to some realistic modern situation in the life of man today.

It is only by such disciplined study, general and particular, that the preacher's mind will be kept full of God's thoughts. He will, no doubt, store up in file or notebooks the treasures which God has unearthed for him. In this way he need never have any fear of his supply drying up or of being left with nothing to preach about. Indeed, there is no chance of it. His problem will rather be how to select his message from such a wealth of available material.

So the skilled steward sees that his larder is kept well stocked. He will never weary the household with a monotonous menu, nor nauseate them with an insipid diet, nor give them indigestion through unsuitable food. The steward will rather be like the householder whom Jesus described, 'who brings out of his treasure what is new and what is old' (Mt. 13:52).

Such is the steward 'of the mysteries of God' — faithful in studying and preaching the Word and in letting men feel the authority of God in and through it; faithful to the householder who has appointed him to the task; faithful to the household who are looking to him for sustenance; and faithful to the deposit which is committed to his trust. May God make us faithful stewards!

CHAPTER TWO

A HERALD

The Preacher's Proclamation and Appeal

IF THE only New Testament metaphor for preaching were that of the steward, we might gain the impression that the preacher's task was a somewhat dull, prosaic and routine affair. But the New Testament is rich in other metaphors, and chief among them is that of the herald charged with the solemn yet exciting responsibility of proclaiming the good news of God. The two are not incompatible. St. Paul thought of himself and his associates in both ways. If at the beginning of 1 Corinthians 4 he says they are 'stewards of the mysteries of God', in the first chapter of the same epistle he sums up the activity of Christian preachers in the phrase 'we preach [*kēryssomen*, we herald] Christ crucified' and declares that it is through this heralded proclamation (*kērygma*) that God is pleased 'to save those who believe' (1 Cor. 1:21, 23). Similarly, in the Pastoral Epistles in which he urges Timothy like a steward both to 'guard the good deposit' and to 'entrust' it 'to faithful men who will be able to teach others also' (2 Tim. 2:2), he twice says that he has been 'appointed a preacher' (*kēryx*, herald) of the gospel (1 Tim. 2:7; 2 Tim. 1:11).

Nevertheless, although the offices of steward and herald are in no way incompatible, they are different, and it may help if I begin by listing the four principal ways in which they should be distinguished.

First, whereas the task of the steward is to feed the household of God, the herald has good news to proclaim to the whole world. This kind of New Testament preaching, says one writer, is not a formal and theoretical discourse 'addressed to a closed group of convinced believers within the precincts of the church', but rather 'a proclamation made by a herald, by the town crier, in the full light of day, to the sound of a trumpet, up-to-the-minute, addressed to everyone because it comes from the king himself'.[1] Several Greek verbs describe this public activity, especially (*an ap di kat*) *aggellein*, 'to declare or to announce' (e.g., Lk. 9:60; 1 John 1:1-5), *euaggelizesthai*, which is not so much our English 'to evangelize' — which is transitive and expects an object — but simply 'to preach good news', and *kēryssein*, 'to proclaim as a herald'. 'The fundamental idea of these words', writes Professor Alan Richardson, 'is the telling of news to people who had not heard it before'.[2]

Secondly, this heralding to outsiders differs from the function of the Christian steward in being rather the proclamation of a deed than the exposition of words, the announcement of God's supernatural intervention, supremely in the death and resurrection of His Son, for the salvation of mankind. As Professor James Stewart has put it; 'Preaching exists, not for the propagating of views, opinions and ideals, but for the proclamation of the mighty acts of God'.[3] I do not mean to imply that these are contradictory. The Christian preacher is both steward and herald. Indeed, the good news he is to herald is contained within the Word of which he is steward, for the Word of God is essentially the record and interpretation of God's great redemptive deed in and through Christ. The Scriptures bear witness to Christ, the only Saviour of sinners. Therefore, a good steward of the

1. Chr. Senft, article 'Preaching' in *Vocabulary of the Bible*, by J. J. von Allmen (London: Lutterworth Press, 1958 [*Vocabulaire Biblique*, 1954]).
2. Richardson, article 'Preach' in *A Theological Word Book of the Bible*, ed. by Alan Richardson (London: S.C.M. Press, 1950).
3. James S. Stewart, *Heralds of God* (London: Hodder & Stoughton, 1946), p. 5.

Word is bound to be also a zealous herald of the good news of salvation in Christ.

We are stewards of what God has said, but heralds of what God has done. Our stewardship is of an accomplished revelation; but an accomplished redemption is the good news which we proclaim as heralds. 'The concept of heralding', Dr. Robert Mounce has written, '. . . is the characteristic way throughout the entire New Testament of referring to the ongoing proclamation of the Christ-event.'[4]

Thirdly, in the stewardship metaphor the emphasis seems to be almost entirely on the activity of the steward and on the requirement that he should be faithful in the guarding and the dispensing of his master's goods; but in the heralding metaphor, activity is expected on the part of the hearers also. The herald does not just preach good news, whether men will hear or whether they will forbear. No. The proclamation issues in an appeal. The herald expects a response. The Christian ambassador, who has announced the reconciliation which God has achieved through Christ, beseeches men to be reconciled to God.

Fourthly, although both steward and herald are go-betweens, the steward standing between householder and household, and the herald between sovereign and people, the herald seems in the New Testament to possess a more direct authority and to represent his master more closely. The steward continues his work even if the householder is far away for long periods; but as the herald issues his proclamation, the voice of the king is heard. The Grimm-Thayer lexicon defines the *kēryx* as 'a herald, a messenger vested with public authority, who conveyed the official messages of kings, magistrates, princes, military commanders, or who gave a public summons or demand. . . .'[5] Thus Christian preachers are 'ambassadors for Christ', as we shall see in greater detail later, 'God making

4. Mounce, *The Essential Nature of New Testament Preaching* (Grand Rapids: Eerdmans, 1960), p. 52.

5. *A Greek-English Lexicon of the New Testament*, 2d ed. rev. (Edinburgh: T. & T. Clark, 1892), p. 346.

his appeal through us' (2 Cor. 5:20). A striking example of this same truth is in the second chapter of the Ephesian Epistle, in which the apostle describes the reconciliation that God has effected both between Jew and Gentile and between them and God. He sums up what Christ has done through His cross in the words 'so making peace'. He then adds: 'And he came and preached peace to you who were far off and peace to those who were near' (Eph. 2:15, 17). This preaching of peace by Jesus Christ (cf. Acts 10:36), according to the context, took place after His death. It can scarcely refer to His teaching during the forty days between the resurrection and the ascension, as in that period He seems to have revealed Himself only to His disciples. It must therefore refer to the work of Christian preachers. The same Christ who once made peace through His cross, now preaches peace through His heralds. It is in this sense that modern writers have described preaching as 'existential'. It is an activity of heralding good news through which God in Christ directly confronts men and women with Himself.

Having briefly suggested the main differences which exist between the concepts of stewarding and heralding, we are in a position to look more closely at the office and work of a herald. In much of this chapter I shall reveal my indebtedness to Professor Robert Mounce, Chairman of the Department of Christianity at Bethel College. His book *The Essential Nature of New Testament Preaching* was published in 1960. As Dr. A. M. Hunter says at the beginning of his Foreword to the book, it 'concerns the *kērygma* — the preached Gospel which the first heralds of Christ proclaimed to the great pagan world of their day, that Gospel which, after nineteen centuries, remains *the* Word from the Beyond for our human predicament'.[6] I have found this book fresh, suggestive and compelling.

'In the world of Homer', writes Dr. Mounce, 'the herald was a man of dignity and held a notable position in the royal

6. Mounce, *op. cit.*, p. 5.

court,' while 'in the post-Homeric era . . . the herald served the state rather than the king'.[7] His task, like the town crier of more recent days, was to make official public proclamations. He needed to have a strong voice and sometimes used a trumpet. Moreover, 'it was essential that the herald be a man of considerable self-control. The proclamation must be delivered exactly as it was received. As the mouthpiece of his master he dare not add his own interpretation'.[8]

Such men are found not infrequently in the Old Testament. Pharaoh caused heralds to precede Joseph's chariot and to cry before him, 'Bow the knee!' (Gen. 41:43). A similar deference was paid to Mordecai as he rode 'on horseback through the open square of the city' (Esther 6:9-11). Nebuchadnezzar's edict that all men should 'fall down and worship the golden image' which he had set up was publicly proclaimed by a herald in the plain of Dura (Dn. 3:1-5). In Judah, as in foreign lands, royal commands were promulgated by heralds, as when King Hezekiah sent couriers throughout Israel and Judah, summoning the people to come to Jerusalem and keep the Passover (2 Chron. 30:1-10).

John the Baptist was such a herald. Some of the minor prophets had made public proclamations in the role of Jehovah's heralds, but in John the Baptist this ministry was clear and unmistakeable. The evangelist Mark identifies him as God's 'messenger' sent to prepare God's way before Him (Mal. 3:1; Mk. 1:2). He was the Messiah's forerunner, calling on the people to repent in order to prepare themselves for the arrival of the Coming One. And if John the Baptist heralded the near approach of the Kingdom of God, Jesus went about proclaiming that with His coming it had in some sense arrived. 'He went about all Galilee, teaching in their synagogues and preaching [*kēryssōn*, heralding] the gospel of the kingdom . . .' (Mt. 4:23). This task He also committed to His disciples. During His lifetime He sent them

7. *Ibid.,* p. 12.
8. *Ibid.,* p. 13.

out, saying, 'Preach [*kēryssete*] as you go, saying "The kingdom of heaven is at hand" ' (Mt. 10:7), and after the Resurrection He gave them His universal commission 'that repentance and forgiveness of sins should be preached [*kērych-
thēnai*] in His name to all nations' (Lk. 24:47).

The Apostolic Kērygma

This brings us to the Acts of the Apostles and to the whole
question of the content of the apostolic *kērygma*. It is well
known that Professor C. H. Dodd, in his book *The Apostolic
Preaching and its Developments*, has drawn a rigid distinction
between the *kērygma* and the *didachē*. The former he defines
as 'the public proclamation of Christianity to the non-Christian world', and the latter as 'ethical instruction' to converts.[9]
Although this differentiation has gained wide acceptance, it
has almost certainly been over-pressed. Dr. Mounce rightly
points out that the verbs *kēryssein*, to herald, and *didaschein*,
to teach, are sometimes used interchangeably in the Gospels,
where one evangelist says Jesus was 'teaching in their synagogues', while another calls it 'preaching in their synagogues'.[10]
The words also overlap in the Acts. So Dr. Mounce writes
of a 'didactic *kērygma*' and says: 'Teaching is the expounding
in detail of that which is proclaimed'.[11] Again, '*Kērygma* is
foundation and *didachē* is superstructure; but no building is
complete without both.'[12]

Accepting, then, that there was a good deal of *didachē*
in the early apostolic *kērygma*, what did these earliest
Christian heralds teach? What was the content of their
proclamation? Professor Dodd's summary of it is that it
was 'a proclamation of the death and resurrection of Jesus
Christ, in an eschatological setting from which those facts

---

9. Dodd, *op. cit.* (London: Willet, 1936), p. 7.
10. E.g., Mt. 4:23 (teaching) =Mk. 1:39 and Lk. 4:44 (preaching);
and Mk. 1:21, 22, 27 (teaching) =1:38 (preaching).
11. Mounce, *op. cit.*, p. 42.
12. *Ibid.*, pp. 42, 43.

derive their saving significance'.[13] Dr. Mounce is justly critical of this also. Affirming that the apostolic *kērygma* was not 'a sort of stereotyped sixheaded sermon'[14] but rather 'a systematic statement of the theology of the primitive church',[15] he suggests that 'in simplest outline' it consisted of three parts, which he summarizes as follows: —

(1) 'A proclamation of the death, resurrection and exaltation of Jesus, seen as the fulfilment of prophecy and involving man's responsibility.

(2) 'The resultant evaluation of Jesus as both Lord and Christ.

(3) 'A summons to repent and receive forgiveness of sins'.[16]

Or, putting the three together, he defines the primitive *kērygma* as 'a proclamation of the death, resurrection and exaltation of Jesus, that led to an evaluation of His person as both Lord and Christ, confronted man with the necessity of repentance, and promised the forgiveness of sins'.[17] The full *kērygma* thus included 'a historical proclamation, a theological evaluation and an ethical summons'.[18] Having made this reconstruction of the *kērygma* from the five speeches of Peter at the beginning of the Acts, Dr. Mounce shows how it is confirmed by what he calls 'a pre-Pauline *kērygma*', as may be deduced from the 'semi-credal elements that are found embedded in the Pauline epistles', which are 'Pre-Pauline' in the sense that they belong to the ' "twilight period" between the founding of the Church and the writing of the Pauline corpus'.[19]

13. Dodd, *op. cit.*, p. 24.
14. Mounce, *op. cit.*, p. 61.
15. *Ibid.*, p. 64.
16. *Ibid.*, p. 77.
17. *Ibid.*, p. 84.
18. *Ibid.*, p. 110.
19. *Ibid.*, p. 88. In his chapter 6, entitled 'Clues to a Pre-Pauline *Kerygma*', pp. 88-109, he examines particularly 1 Cor. 15:3ff.; Rom. 10:9; Rom. 1:3, 4; Rom. 4:24, 25; Rom. 8:34; 1 Cor. 11:23ff. and Phil. 2:6-11.

For our more practical purpose in this chapter I think we may even further simplify Dr. Mounce's excellent summary of the apostolic *kērygma*. Fundamentally, it consisted of only two parts, which we may perhaps call 'proclamation' and 'appeal'. The first comprises both (1) and (2) of Dr. Mounce's summary. It concerns both the work of Jesus Christ and the consequent evaluation of His person. It is a proclamation of Him as Saviour and Lord. This, surely, is still the irreducible minimum of the gospel. To preach the gospel is to preach Christ, for Christ *is* the gospel (e.g., Acts 8:5; Phil. 1:15). But how shall we preach Him? We shall preach Him as Lord (2 Cor. 4:5), the Lord from heaven, exalted at the Father's right hand, to whom men owe allegiance. We shall also preach Him as the crucified Saviour, 'who was put to death for our trespasses and raised for our justification' (Rom. 4:25). These are the two essential parts of the heralding of Christ. They concern His divine Person and His saving work: —

> *kēryssomen Christon estaurōmenon*
> (1 Cor. 1:23 — 'We preach . . . Christ crucified')
> *kēryssomen . . . Christon . . . Kurion*
> (2 Cor. 4:5 — ' We preach . . . Christ as Lord')

It has often been said that the emphasis of the early sermons in the Acts, and therefore of the primitive *kērygma*, was upon the resurrection of Jesus, rather than upon His death, and that Luke gives a concise statement of their message when he says that Paul 'preached Jesus and the resurrection' (Acts 17:18). This is true and yet can be misleading. They did not preach the resurrection in isolation, but in relation to the death which preceded it and the ascension which followed. Thus the resurrection was 'the most central of the three great events that formed the historical foundation of the *kērygma*'.[20] Nevertheless, there can be no question that, although Christ's saving career is one, it is principally by His *death* that men

---

20. Mounce, *op. cit.*, p. 78.

may be saved. We read in I Cor. 15:3ff. (which Dr. Mounce calls 'without doubt the most valuable piece of pre-Pauline Christianity in the New Testament' and even 'the oldest document of the Christian Church in existence'[21]) that 'Christ *died* for our sins', not that 'Christ *rose* for our sins'. Certainly the Apostle goes on in this primitive statement of the gospel to say 'He was raised' and that 'He appeared' to various chosen witnesses, but His resurrection did not in itself accomplish our salvation, but rather gave public evidence of its accomplishment by Christ's death, with which the Father was well pleased. That is why Paul can write later in the same chapter: 'If Christ has not been raised, then our preaching is in vain and your faith is in vain. . . . If Christ has not been raised, your faith is futile and you are still in your sins' (1 Cor. 15:14, 17). If Jesus never rose from the dead, men are still unsaved sinners, not because the resurrection would have saved them, but because without the resurrection the death of Jesus is shown to have been without saving efficacy.

That is why 'we preach Christ crucified' is the heart of the gospel. We also preach Christ born and living on earth (since He could not have been our Saviour if He had not been made flesh and lived a sinless life). We also preach Christ risen and exalted (since by His resurrection He was publicly vindicated and by His exaltation He became our present mediator). But the emphasis in the New Testament *kērygma* is on the Saviour's atoning death for the sins of the world. Well may we echo Paul's affirmation: 'I decided to know nothing among you except Jesus Christ and Him crucified' (1 Cor. 2:2).

The first part of our simplified *kērygma*, then, is the proclamation of Jesus as Saviour and Lord. The second part is the appeal to men and women to come to Him in repentance and faith. The definition of evangelism originally prepared in 1918 by the Archbishops' Committee of Enquiry on the Evangelistic Work of the Church, and subsequently

21. *Ibid.,* pp. 90, 91.

adopted (with slight alterations) by the Department of Evangelism of the World Council of Churches, does not say, 'to evangelize is to present Christ Jesus', but, 'to evangelize is *so* to present Christ Jesus . . . that men shall come to put their trust in God through Him, to accept Him as their Saviour and serve Him as their King. . .'.[22] In other words, true evangelism seeks a response. It expects results. It is preaching for a verdict. Heralding is not the same as lecturing. A lecture is dispassionate, objective, academic. It is addressed to the mind. It seeks no result but to impart certain information and, perhaps, to provoke the student to further enquiry. But the herald of God comes with an urgent proclamation of peace through the blood of the cross, and with a summons to men to repent, to lay down their arms and humbly to accept the offered pardon.

Ambassadors for Christ

This distinction between proclamation and appeal in the work of the herald is nowhere elaborated more fully than in 2 Corinthians 5:18-21. It is true that the words for 'herald' and 'heralding' do not occur in these verses, but the idea is quite clearly present. It is here that Paul says 'we are ambassadors for Christ', and there is really no difference between the functions of the 'ambassador' and the 'herald'. 'I most sincerely congratulate you," wrote Charles Simeon to John Venn on the occasion of his ordination in 1782, "not on a permission to receive 40 or 50 pounds a year, nor on the title of Reverend, but on your accession to the most valuable, most honorable, most important, and most glorious office in the world — to that of an ambassador of the Lord Jesus Christ.'[23] Before looking at the passage in 2 Corinthians 5 closely, we must pause to examine the word for 'we are ambassadors' (*presbeuomen*).

---

22. "Towards the Conversion of England," Press and Publications Board of the Church Assembly (1945), p. 1.
23. William Carus, *Memoirs of the Life of the Rev. Charles Simeon* (London: Hatchard, 1847), p. 28.

It stems from *presbus,* an old man or an elder. *Presbeia,* therefore, meant first age or seniority. But it came to be applied to the dignity and rank which belong to seniority or precedence. Hence, according to the Grimm-Thayer lexicon, it was used for 'the business wont to be intrusted to elders, specially the office of an ambassador'.[24] Moulton and Milligan state that this word was 'in everyday use in the intercourse between the Greek cities and between them and the kings'.[25] The man holding this office was called the *presbeus* or *presbeutēs,* which was equivalent to the Latin *legatus,*[26] while his activity was described by the word *presbeuein.* This, say Moulton and Milligan, 'was the regular word in the Greek East for the Emperor's legate',[27] that is, his personal representative, who was often the governor of a province.

These words occur several times in the First Book of the Maccabees[28] and also in the canonical books of the Septuagint —for instance, when 'envoys' were sent by the princes of Babylon to Hezekiah (2 Chron. 32:31). But in the New Testament the noun *presbeia,* embassy, occurs only twice, and the verb *presbeuein,* to act as an ambassador, twice also. The two occurrences of *presbeia* are in parables of Jesus recorded by St. Luke. In the Parable of the Pounds, when the 'nobleman went into a far country to receive kingly power and then return', 'his citizens . . . sent an embassy after him, saying, "We do not want this man to reign over us" ' (Lk. 19:12-14). In the Parable of the King Marching to Battle, Jesus suggests that, when he discovers that the other king has an army twice the size of his, 'he sends an embassy and asks terms of peace' (Lk. 14:31, 32). Both occurrences of the verb *presbeuein*

24. Grimm-Thayer, *op. cit.,* p. 535.
25. *The Vocabulary of the Greek Testament* (Grand Rapids: Eerdmans), p. 534.
26. Cf. the relation between our English words 'embassy' and 'legation'.
27. *Loc. cit.*
28. *Presbeutes* in 1 Macc. 13:21, 14:21, 22 and *presbeus* in 1 Macc. 9:70, 11:9 and 13:14.

are from the pen of St. Paul. At the end of his Epistle to
the Ephesians he describes himself as 'an ambassador in chains'
on behalf of the gospel (Eph. 6:20).[29] He was an ambassador
for the gospel, heralding its good news, proclaiming its offer
of peace, and it was on account of this that he found himself
a prisoner now. The other use of the verb *presbeuein* comes
in 2 Corinthians 5:18-21, to a detailed study of which we
must now turn.

> All this is from God, who through Christ reconciled us to Himself
> and gave us the ministry of reconciliation; that is, God was in
> Christ, reconciling the world to Himself, not counting their
> trespasses against them, and entrusting to us the message of
> reconciliation. So we are ambassadors for Christ, God making His
> appeal through us. We beseech you on behalf of Christ, be recon-
> ciled to God. For our sake He made Him to be sin who knew no
> sin, so that in Him we might become the righteousness of God.

This passage treats salvation in terms of reconciliation,
which, according to Vincent Taylor, is 'the best New Testament word to describe the purpose of the Atonement'. It
is certainly the most homely and personal word, where the
sacrificial, commercial and judicial ideas involved in propitiation, redemption and justification may sound foreign and
unfamiliar to modern ears. In treating this great theme, the
Apostle proceeds in two stages. First, he makes his proclamation of how the reconciliation has been accomplished by God
through Christ. Then, calling himself an ambassador, he issues
his appeal to men to be reconciled to God.

The Proclamation

We shall take the proclamation first. He begins 'all this is
from God' (v. 15). God is the author of the reconciliation.
The initiative in the work of atonement has been taken by
the Father; it is not man's. In Archbishop William Temple's
lucid phrase, 'All is of God. The only thing of my very
own which I contribute to my redemption is the sin from

29. Cf. v. 15, 'the gospel of peace'.

which I need to be redeemed'. Nor is the initiative Christ's. The reconciliation is 'through Christ' (v. 18) and 'in Christ' (v. 19) but 'from [*ek*] God' (v. 18). Jesus Christ is the means through whom, but not the source from whom, the reconciliation comes. Any explanation of the atonement which suggests that the saving initiative lay with the Son rather than with the Father, or that the Father was 'the object of some third party's intervention in reconciling'[30] must be ruthlessly rejected as unBiblical. We cannot tolerate the idea that there was any reluctance in the Father. On the contrary, 'God . . . reconciled us to Himself' (v. 18). In order to put this beyond all dispute, seven main verbs in this sentence (whether indicatives or participles) have God as their subject. It is God who reconciled, who gave, who was in Christ reconciling, who did not impute our sins to us, who entrusted to us the message of reconciliation, who makes His appeal to men, who made Christ to be sin. The desire, the thought, the plan, the means to reconcile are 'all . . . from God'.

But if the author of the reconciliation is God, the agent is Christ. It is 'through Christ' and 'in Christ' that God has accomplished the reconciliation. And He has done it objectively and decisively. This is clear from the aorist participle *katallaxantos* in verse 18. Full force must be given to it. Here is something not which God is doing, but which God did. To quote P. T. Forsyth again, God was 'actually reconciling, finishing the work. It was not a tentative, preliminary affair. . . . Reconciliation was finished in Christ's death. Paul did not preach a gradual reconciliation. He preached what the old divines used to call the finished work. . . . He preached something done once for all — a reconciliation which is the base of every soul's reconcilement, not an invitation only'.[31] Similarly, James Denney

---

30. P. T. Forsyth, *The Work of Christ* (London: Hodder & Stoughton, 1910) , p. 89.

31. Forsyth, *op. cit.,* p. 86.

wrote, 'The work of reconciliation, in the sense of the New Testament, is a work which is *finished*, and which we must conceive to be finished, *before the gospel is preached*'.[32]

This objective achievement of God through Christ's cross is indicated by something more than the aorist participle *katallaxantos*. It is made plain by the contrast between the 'reconciling' verbs in verses 18 and 19 on the one hand and in verse 20 on the other. We must find some explanation of the words 'God . . . reconciled us to Himself' (v. 18) and 'God was in Christ reconciling the world to Himself' (v. 19), which still does full justice to verse 20 'be reconciled to God'. If we interpret the first two verbs as referring to God's present reconciling influence on men, the appeal of verse 20 is evacuated of its meaning and we have succeeded in making nonsense of the whole passage. It is clear that there is a difference here which must be preserved. The two stages must not be confused. We must distinguish between the divine initiative in Christ's death and the divine appeal leading to man's response today. The first was an achievement (expressed by the aorist participle *katallaxantos*, v.18); the second is an appeal (expressed by the aorist imperative *katallagēte*, v. 20).

What was this achievement? What has God done in and through Christ to deal with our sins (upon which His wrath abides) and so to remove the barrier which separates us from Him and to reconcile us to Himself? First, and negatively, He has refused to impute our sins to us (v. 19). The phrase is taken from Psalms 32:2 (quoted in Rom. 4:8), where the blessedness of the man to whom God does not impute iniquity is described. The words imply that it would have been natural and lawful for God to have imputed our sins to us. True, 'sin is not imputed when there is no law' (Rom. 5:13, A.V.), but when there is a law, sins (here rightly called 'trespasses') are and must be imputed. That is,

32. James Denney, *The Death of Christ,* 1902 (London: Tyndale Press, 1950) , p. 85.

they are reckoned as the sinner's responsibility and counted against him. But it is just this which God in His sheer grace has refused to do. He has declined to lay them to our charge. Instead, and this is the second and positive action Paul says God has taken, God 'for our sake . . . made Him to be sin who knew no sin, so that in Him we might become the righteousness of God' (v. 21). These wonderful words are acknowledged as forming one of the most daring phrases in the New Testament about the death of Christ. One inevitably associates it with Galatians 3:13, where it is written that Christ was made 'a curse for us'. What did Paul mean by it?

The verse (21) opens with a declaration of Christ's sinlessness. He is not identified by name, but there is only one Person who answers to the description, 'who knew no sin'. He 'knew' it not in the Hebrew sense of the verb. He had no experience of sin whatever. It is this sinless Christ who was made sin. What can this possibly mean except that He was made sin with our sins? Paul is not suggesting merely that Jesus Christ had a deep, sympathetic fellow-feeling with us in our sins; he is rather indicating Christ's real and terrible identification with us in our sins — an identification for which His own personal separation from sin uniquely fitted Him.[33] Having been 'made flesh' in the womb of Mary His mother, He was 'made sin' on the cross of Calvary. God who would not impute our trespasses to us, imputed them instead to Christ, and made His sinless Son to be sin for our sake. In saying this, we do not forget what verse 19 teaches, namely, that 'God was in Christ reconciling the world to Himself'. How God can have been in Christ when He made Christ to be sin, I cannot say. We are here touching the ultimate paradox of the atonement. But Paul taught both, and we hold both, even if we cannot satisfactorily reconcile them or

33. The link in apostolic thought and teaching between Christ's sinlessness and His death for our sins may also be seen in Heb. 7:26, 27; 1 Pet. 1:18, 19, 2:22, 24, 3:18 and 1 John 3:5.

neatly formulate them. God made Christ to be sin with our sins, so that we might become righteous with His righteousness. This mysterious exchange is possible only to those who are 'in Him' (the last two words of the chapter), who are personally united to Christ by faith. God was in Christ to achieve our reconciliation (v. 19); we must be in Christ to receive it (v. 21).

It should be evident, therefore, that the reconciliation is not just the overcoming of man's stubborn resistance, but the bearing of man's sin and condemnation. The 'change' is in God also and not in man.[34] It is true that the New Testament never says in precise words that God is or has been reconciled to man; that He is never the object of the verb 'to reconcile'; and that when He is the subject, the verb is always active and not passive. Nevertheless, Dean J. H. Bernard writes about the idea of God being reconciled to us: 'That St. Paul would have felt any difficulty in such a phrase is very unlikely'.[35] What is certain is that the apostle Paul presents the reconciliation as a divine achievement, through the death of Christ and independent of man's contribution, which we have but to 'receive' (Rom. 5:11) as a free gift. To quote James Denney again, 'It is in virtue of something already consummated on His cross that Christ is able to make the appeal to us which He does, and to win the response in which we *receive* the reconciliation'.[36]

It is this reconciliation which we are called to proclaim as heralds. If the author of the reconciliation is God and the agent of the reconciliation is Christ, men are its ambassadors. This is the sequence of thought. The reconciliation comes from God through Christ to us, first to receive it ourselves

34. Dr. Leon Morris in Chapter VI of his *The Apostolic Preaching of the Cross* (Grand Rapids: Eerdmans, 1955) argues that the idea of 'change' is the basic significance of *allasso*, 'reconcile', and its compounds. He also gives Rabbinic examples, one reference from Josephus and three from 2 Maccabees, in which God is said to be reconciled to man.

35. An *Expositor's Greek Testament,* ed. W. R. Nicoll (Grand Rapids: Eerdmans), *ad loc.*

36. Denney, *op. cit.,* p. 86.

and then to make it known to others. God is not satisfied when He has devised our reconciliation, effected it and bestowed it; He makes provision also for its promulgation. Those who proclaim it are to be those who have received it. So God gives us two gifts, first the reconciliation itself, and then 'the ministry' (v. 18) and 'the message' (v. 19) of reconciliation. Until we have received the reconciliation, we cannot proclaim it; once we have received it, we must. Or, to put the same truth in different words, once we are 'in Christ' and have become God's righteousness (v. 21), we find that we are 'for Christ' and have become His ambassadors (v. 20). Moreover, it is not unimportant to notice that in both expressions 'the ministry of reconciliation' (v. 18) and 'the message of reconciliation' (v. 19), 'reconciliation' has the definite article. It is to the ministry of *the* reconciliation that we have been called. It is the message of *the* reconciliation that we must proclaim. We are commissioned to be heralds of the one and only reconciliation of which Paul has been writing, and which was accomplished by the Father through the Son on the cross.

Thus the apostle Paul sets forth what we have called the proclamation, the announcement of what God has done for our reconciliation to Himself. He has refused to impute our sins to us. He has made Christ to be sin for us. This is the 'gospel' of which we are heralds. It is the proclamation of a fact, of a deed which is gloriously done and absolutely finished, of a gift which may now be freely received. But, precious as this good news is, we cannot remain indifferent to our hearers' response to it. So Paul proceeds from the proclamation to the appeal. 'We are ambassadors for Christ,' he writes, 'God making His appeal through us. We beseech you on behalf of Christ, be reconciled to God' (v. 20).

The Appeal

The ambassador's appeal is represented in two ways here. First, it is '*we* are ambassadors for Christ . . . *we* beseech you on behalf of Christ'. Secondly, it is '*God* making *His* appeal through us'. We shall study both these expressions in turn.

First, 'we are ambassadors for Christ . . . we beseech you on behalf of Christ'. The repetition of *huper Christou* ('for' or 'on behalf of' Christ) is wonderful indeed. This is our high privilege. It was 'for our sake' (*huper hēmōn*, v. 21) that God made Christ to be sin; it is now for Christ's sake (*huper Christou*, v. 20) that God makes us ambassadors. His concern for us was so great that it led to the cross; how much concern have we for Christ? If we loved Him as much as He loved us, we should be zealous ambassadors indeed! This 'for Christ's sake' could transform our ministry. There is no more powerful incentive in evangelism than *huper tou onomatos autou*, 'for the sake of His [or simply 'the'] Name' (Rom. 1:5).[37]

> All may of Thee partake;
> Nothing can be so mean
> Which, with this tincture, *for Thy sake*,
> Will not grow bright and clean.
> —George Herbert
> 1593-1632

It is, then, for Christ's sake, for the spread of His Kingdom and the glory of His Name, that we are ambassadors and beseech men to be reconciled to God. We cannot bear to think that He may have suffered in vain. Has God in and through the death of Christ done all that is necessary for man's reconciliation? Then we shall spare no pains to urge upon men, persistently, earnestly, the necessity of being reconciled to God. Such an urgent appeal is not popular in certain church circles today, but I have no doubt that this is what St. Paul meant, and I hope to prove it.

St. Paul uses two verbs to describe the ambassador's appeal, 'God making His appeal', which is *parakalountos*, and 'we

---

37. For the same incentive in suffering rather than service cf. Acts 5:41; Phil. 1:29.

beseech you', which is *deometha*. *Parakalein* is a word with a wide variety of uses, particularly 'admonish, exhort', 'beg, entreat, beseech',[38] as well as meaning to comfort, to encourage and to strengthen. But *deomai* is less ambiguous. True, it is often quite weak (as e.g., in Acts 8:34, 21:39, 26:3), but it really signifies, to 'ask, beg, entreat, beseech, implore'. In St. Luke's Gospel it is used of the leper who, 'when he saw Jesus, fell on his face and *besought* him' for cleansing (Lk. 5:12); of the Gadarene demoniac who first fell down before Jesus and with a loud voice cried, 'I *beseech* you, do not torment me', and later '*begged* that he might be with Him' (Lk. 8:28, 38); and of the father of the apparently epileptic boy who had '*begged*' the disciples to cast out the unclean spirit and now cried to Jesus, 'Teacher, I *beg* you to look upon my son' (Lk. 9:38, 40). This is the verb also which St. Paul used in some of the more personal and emotional passages in his epistles (e.g., Gal. 4:12; 2 Cor. 10:2 [v. 1 is *parakalein*]). It is this word also which is used of prayer. Sometimes, indeed, it refers to ordinary petition, (e.g., Mt. 9:38 = Lk. 10:2; Lk. 21:36, 22:32; Acts 4:31, 8:22, 24; 1 Thess. 3:10), but sometimes *deēsis* means strong supplication, as when Jesus agonized in the Garden of Gethsemane (Heb. 5:7), or when the apostle expresses his 'heart's desire and prayer [*deēsis*] to God' for Israel 'that they may be saved' (Rom. 10:1, cf. 9:1-3). In the light of this New Testament usage it is legitimate to see in the ambassador's appeal a most urgent entreaty to men to get right with God. Nothing less fervent would be appropriate to one who labours 'on behalf of Christ' and Him crucified.

The second way in which the apostle describes the appeal is even more striking. It is not only, he declares, that '*we* are ambassadors for Christ' and that '*we* beseech' people to be reconciled to God; it is also that *God* is 'making *His* appeal through us'. The same God who effected the reconciliation and gave us the ministry and the message of recon-

38. Grimm-Thayer, *op. cit.*, pp. 482-483.

ciliation yet retains the initiative in this last stage of the
process also. As the achievement was His, so the appeal is
His too. We need to ponder the divine condescension. He
who once worked *'for* us' (v. 21, A.V.) now works *'through*
us' (v. 20). Indeed, He who acted 'through *Christ*' (v. 18)
to accomplish the reconciliation now acts 'through *us*' (v.
20) to implore sinners to accept it. Whereas *Christ* was His
agent in the one, *we* are His agents in the other. Such is
the unspeakable honour which He confers upon His ambassadors. It is as if He uses the heralding of the good news,
both in the proclamation and in the appeal, to speak to men
Himself, to manifest Himself to them and to bring them to
salvation.

There is need for caution in the way in which this tremen-
dous truth is stated. Modern writers have been so anxious
to draw attention to what they call 'the existential nature of
preaching'[39] that they seem to me to be in danger of going
too far. In Dr. Mounce's last chapter, which he entitles 'The
Essential Nature of Preaching', he writes: 'The proclamation
of the cross is itself the continuance, or extension in time,
of that very redemptive act'.[40] 'It prolongs and mediates
the redemptive activity of God'.[41] 'As he [the preacher]
by faith proclaims the great Act of God, he realizes that
it is once again taking place'.[42] 'The barriers of time are
somehow transcended and that supreme event of the past is
once again taking place'.[43] Similarly, in the Preface to his
book, he writes: 'Standing at the crossroads of time and
eternity, he [the preacher] has the exalted privilege to prolong in time that mighty act of God which in one sense belongs to a specific date in the Roman Imperial Age'.[44] I confess that I find some of this language loose and perilous. In

39. R. Mounce, *op. cit.,* p. 153.
40. *Ibid.,* pp. 153, 154.
41. *Ibid.,* p. 155.
42. *Ibid.,* p. 159.
43. *Ibid.,* p. 153.
44. *Ibid.,* p. 7.

what sense can the herald by his proclamation 'prolong' or effect an 'extension' or 'continuance' of God's redemptive act in the cross? Dr. Mounce seems to indicate that in some way the cross is 'once again taking place'. At least he uses this expression twice. But I feel confident that he does not mean that there is or could be any repetition of the Saviour's atoning death. Christ died *hapax*, once and for all, as the New Testament writers say again and again. His work was finished, His sacrifice complete, His task done on the cross and, 'after He had offered one sacrifice for sins for ever' (Heb. 10:12, A.V.), He sat down at the Father's right hand.

What Dr. Mounce and other writers are really saying, I believe — with which I heartily agree — is that it is by preaching that God makes past history a present reality. The cross was, and will always remain, a unique historical event of the past. And there it will remain, in the past, in the books, unless God Himself makes it real and relevant to men today. It is by preaching, in which He makes His appeal to men through men, that God accomplishes this miracle. He opens their eyes to see its true meaning, its eternal value and its abiding merit. 'Preaching,' writes Dr. Mounce, 'is that time-less link between God's great redemptive Act and man's apprehension of it. It is the medium through which God contemporizes His historic Self-disclosure and offers man the opportunity to respond in faith.'[45] But it is more even than this. God not only *confronts* men through the preacher's proclamation; He actually *saves* men through it as well. This St. Paul states categorically: 'Since, in the wisdom of God, the world did not know God through wisdom, it pleased God through the folly of the *kērygma* to save those who believe' (1 Cor. 1:21). Similarly, the gospel is itself 'the power of God unto salvation to every one that believeth' (Rom. 1:16, A.V.). Did not Jesus in the Nazareth Synagogue, quoting from Isaiah 61, say: 'The Spirit of the Lord is upon me, because He has anointed me to preach good news to the

45. *Ibid.*, p. 153.

poor. He has sent me to proclaim release to the captives and recovering of sight to the blind, to set at liberty those who are oppressed'? (Lk. 4:18). His mission, He says, is not only 'to proclaim release to the captives' but actually 'to set' them 'at liberty'! 'Herein,' comments Dr. Mounce, 'lies a uniqueness that characterizes New Testament heralding: while it proclaims, it brings to pass its proclamation. The proclamation of liberty at the same time frees. The preaching of sight opens blind eyes.'[46]

All this does not mean that the cross and the preaching of the cross are two comparable parts of God's redemption. Away with the thought! God has accomplished our redemption at the cross; preaching 'effectively communicates the power and redemptive activity of God'.[47] Or, returning to 2 Corinthians 5, God has reconciled us to Himself through Christ; what He does through us is to appeal to men to be reconciled to Him and thus to draw them into an enjoyment of the reconciliation.

It is now time to conclude with a practical application of all this theory. The great lesson the herald metaphor can teach us, as it is used in the New Testament, is that proclamation and appeal belong together. We must not separate them. One without the other makes true New Testament preaching impossible. We find them wedded in many places. One example is our Lord's first recorded words in the public ministry: 'The time is fulfilled, and the kingdom of God is at hand [which is proclamation]; repent, and believe in the gospel [which is appeal]' (Mk. 1:15). Another instance is in the Parable of the Great Feast, where the servant is instructed to say to those who have been invited: 'Come; for all is now ready' (Lk. 14:17). 'All is now ready' is the proclamation; 'Come' is the consequent appeal. The same pattern may be discerned in the early speeches of the Acts, for example: 'God . . . glorified His servant Jesus, whom you

46. *Ibid.,* p. 18.
47. *Ibid.,* p. 155.

delivered up . . . you . . . killed the Author of life, whom God raised from the dead. . . . Repent therefore . . .' (Acts 3:13-19). Again, we have clearly discovered this sequence in Paul's Second Letter to the Corinthians: first came the announcement of the achieved reconciliation; then the appeal to receive it. First, in effect, 'God is reconciled to you'; then 'be ye reconciled to God'.

No Appeal without Proclamation

From this coupling together of proclamation and appeal, we may learn two complementary lessons. First, we must never issue an appeal without first making the proclamation. Much harm has been done to the souls of men, and much dishonour brought to the name of Christ, through neglect of this simple rule. Evangelistic preaching has too often consisted of a prolonged appeal for decision when the congregation has been given no substance upon which the decision is to be made. But the gospel is not fundamentally an invitation to men to do anything. It is a declaration of what God has done in Christ on the cross for their salvation. The invitation cannot properly be given before the declaration has been made. Men must grasp the truth before they are asked to respond to it. It is true that man's intellect is finite and fallen, but he must never be asked to murder it. If he comes to Jesus Christ in repentance and faith, it must be with the full consent of his mind. Much of the leakage of converts after evangelistic campaigns is due to the evangelist's disregard of this. If it be said that we cannot consider man's mind in our evangelistic preaching because it is darkened, I can only reply that the apostles were of a different opinion. Some of the verbs which Luke uses in the Acts to describe the apostles' preaching are decidedly intellectual, i.e. *didaschein* (teach), *dialegesthai* (argue), *suzētein* (dispute), *sunchunein* (confound), *paratithēmi* and *sumbibazein* (prove), *diakatalegkein* (confute powerfully) (see Acts 20:31, 17:2, 17, 18:4, 19, 19:8, 9, 24:25, 9:29, 9:22, 17:3, 9:22, 18:28).

Sometimes, too, as a result of this didactic preaching, we read not that people were 'converted', but that they were 'persuaded' (Acts 17:4, 18:4, 19:8, 26, 28:23, 24). What does this mean? It means that the apostles were teaching a body of doctrine and arguing towards a conclusion. They sought to make an intellectual conquest, to persuade men of the truth of their message, to convince them in order to convert them. This interesting fact is further confirmed by two other considerations. The first is that Paul sometimes stayed for long periods in one place. The most notable example is his visit to Ephesus on the third missionary journey. After three months' ministry in the synagogue, he withdrew and 'argued daily in the hall of Tyrannus [some manuscripts add "from the fifth hour to the tenth"] . . . for two years' (Acts 19:8-10 ; cf. 14:3, 16:12, 14, 18:11, 18). A daily five-hour lecture throughout two years! That works out at over 25,000 hours of gospel teaching! No wonder we read in verse 10 that, as a result, 'all the residents of Asia heard the word of the Lord, both Jews and Greeks'. There is no doubt that the early apostolic *kērygma* was full of solid *didachē*.[48] The second confirmation of the fact that there was intellectual body in the gospel preaching of the apostles is that in the New Testament the conversion experience is frequently expressed in terms of response not to Christ but to 'the truth'. It is 'believing the truth' (2 Thess. 2:10-13), 'acknowledging the truth' (2 Tim. 2:25, Tit. 1:1), 'obeying the truth' (Rom. 2:8; 1 Pet. 1:22; cf. Gal. 5:7) and 'coming to know the truth' (John 8:32; 1 Tim. 2:4, 4:3; 1 John 2:21), while the preaching itself is 'the open statement of the truth' (2 Cor. 4:2). Paul even goes so far as to describe to the Romans their conversion in these words: 'You . . . have become obedient from the heart to the standard of teaching [*tupon didachēs*] to which you were committed' (Rom. 6:17).

48. See Acts 13:12 and 17:19, where the gospel preaching is actually called *didache,* and, e.g., 5:42, 28:31, where 'preaching' and 'teaching' certainly cannot mean simply teaching the converted and preaching to the unconverted.

So we must follow the apostles' example and not be afraid either to teach people solid doctrine or to reason with them. Of course they can neither understand nor believe without the illumination of the Holy Spirit, but this does not mean we are at liberty to dilute the intellectual content of the gospel. As Gresham Machen has wisely said, we must do our utmost to give people good reasons why they should believe, but it is the Holy Spirit who opens their minds to 'attend to the evidence'.[49]

No Proclamation without Appeal

The second lesson we must learn from this Biblical coupling together of proclamation and appeal is the complementary one: we must never make the proclamation without then issuing an appeal. If one had to choose between the two, I would rather have the proclamation than the appeal, but fortunately we are not faced with this choice. We are to find room for both proclamation and appeal in our preaching if we would be true heralds of the King. I am not presuming to say what form the appeal should take. Nor am I advocating any particular evangelistic technique or method. I am simply saying that proclamation without appeal is not Biblical preaching. It is not enough to teach the gospel; we must urge men to embrace it.

Naturally, there are many factors which inhibit preachers from making this appeal. There is a kind of hyper-Calvinism, which regards the call to repentance and faith as an attempt to usurp the prerogatives of the Holy Spirit. Of course we agree that man is blind, dead and bound; that repentance and faith are the gifts of God; and that men are unable to turn from their sins to Christ without the prevenient grace of the Holy Spirit. The apostle Paul taught these truths. But this should not stop us from beseeching men to be reconciled to God, for the apostle Paul did this also! Other preachers

49. J. Gresham Machen, *Christian Faith in the Modern World* (Grand Rapids: Eerdmans), p. 630.

have a great horror of emotionalism. So have I, if this means the artificial stirring of the emotions by rhetorical tricks or other devices. But we should not fear genuine emotion. If we can preach Christ crucified and remain altogether unmoved, we must have a hard heart indeed. More to be feared than emotion is cold professionalism, the dry, detached utterance of a lecture which has neither heart nor soul in it. Do man's peril and Christ's salvation mean so little to us that we feel no warmth rise within us as we think about them? Very different was Richard Baxter, who wrote in his *Reformed Pastor* (1656): 'I marvel how I can preach . . . slightly and coldly, how I can let men alone in their sins and that I do not go to them and beseech them for the Lord's sake to repent, however they take it and whatever pains or trouble it should cost me. I seldom come out of the pulpit but my conscience smiteth me that I have been no more serious and fervent. It accuseth me not so much for want of human ornaments or elegance, nor for letting fall an uncomely word; but it asketh me: "How could'st thou speak of life and death with such a heart? Should'st thou not weep over such a people, and should not thy tears interrupt thy words? Should'st not thou cry aloud and shew them their transgressions and entreat and beseech them as for life and death?"[50]

So the true herald of God is careful first to make a thorough and thoughtful proclamation of God's great deed of redemption through Christ's cross, and then to issue a sincere and earnest appeal to men to repent and believe. Not one without the other, but both.

> Thy heralds brought glad tidings
>   To greatest, as to least;
> They bade men rise, and hasten
>   To share the great king's feast. . . .

50. Richard Baxter, *The Reformed Pastor* (London: Epworth Press, 2nd ed. rev., 1950), pp. 145, 106.

Their gospel of redemption,
  Sin pardoned, man restored,
Was all in this enfolded:
  One Church, one faith, one Lord.

And we, shall we be faithless?
  Shall hearts fail, hands hang down?
Shall we evade the conflict,
  And cast away our crown?
Not so: in God's deep counsels
  Some better thing is stored;
We will maintain, unflinching,
  One Church, one faith, one Lord.

            —E. H. Plumptre, 1821-1891

CHAPTER THREE

A WITNESS

The Preacher's Experience and Humility

THE third word used in the New Testament for the Christian preacher is the word 'witness'. To be sure, it is possible to be a witness to our Lord Jesus Christ without being a preacher, but all the same the activity of preaching is sometimes described as 'testifying'. For instance, addressing the Ephesian elders at Miletus, Paul describes the ministry which he had 'received from the Lord Jesus', as 'to testify to the gospel of the grace of God' and again, 'testifying both to Jews and to Greeks of repentance to God and of faith in our Lord Jesus Christ (Acts 20:24, 31).

I wonder what the words 'witness' and 'testify' suggest to your mind? To some they signify what is commonly called 'giving a testimony', which usually seems to mean narrating the circumstances of one's conversion and perhaps adding a brief autobiographical sketch of one's subsequent spiritual pilgrimage. To others 'witness' refers supremely to the testimony of our lives rather than of our lips, and means the powerful influence of a Christian example. There is truth in both these views, inasmuch as our spoken witness must be corroborated on the one hand by the authority of personal experience, and on the other by the evidence of a consistent life. Nevertheless, the concept of 'witness' in Scripture is considerably wider than either of these two ideas, and it is important to think of the preacher as a 'witness' against the background of the whole scriptural teaching on the subject. I do not think we could do better than take for the basis of our thinking the words of Jesus recorded in John 15:26, 27 (A.V.): 'But when the Comforter is come, whom I will send unto

you from the Father, even the Spirit of truth, which proceedeth from the Father, he shall testify of me: and ye also
shall bear witness, because ye have been with me from the
beginning'.

The words 'testify' and 'witness' introduce us to a situation
quite different from those which we have been considering
in the two previous chapters. 'Steward' is a domestic metaphor. It takes us into a house, where we think of a householder entrusting his steward with certain stores for the well-
being of the household. 'Herald' is a political metaphor. It
takes us into the open air, perhaps a market place or street
corner, where the herald sounds his trumpet to gather the
people together and then, on behalf of his king, makes an
urgent proclamation of glad tidings. But 'witness' is a legal
metaphor. It takes us into the lawcourts. We see the judge
on his bench and the prisoner on trial in the dock. We hear
the case argued by barristers, first the prosecution, then the
defence, who call witnesses to substantiate what they say.

In what sense, then, is the preacher in the New Testament
called a 'witness' and expected to 'testify'? I suggest that the
situation envisaged is this: Jesus Christ stands on trial, not
now before the Sanhedrin, before Pontius Pilate the procurator
or Herod Antipas, but at the bar of world opinion. The
'world', which in biblical language means secular, godless,
non-Christian society, now uncommitted, now hostile, is
in the role of judge. The world is judging Jesus continuously,
passing its various verdicts upon Him. The devil accuses
Him with many ugly lies and musters his false witnesses by the
hundred. The Holy Spirit is the *Paraklētos*, the counsel for
the defence, and He calls us to be witnesses to substantiate His
case. Christian preachers are privileged to testify to and
for Jesus Christ, defending Him, commending Him, bringing
before the court evidence which they must hear and consider before they return their verdict.

Let us now examine in detail this brief summary.

First, Christian witness is borne before the world. It is
'the world' before whom Jesus is arraigned and by whom

He is being judged, and the preacher's witness cannot be understood or appreciated until we have a truly biblical understanding of the world. We need to study the Johannine literature if we would discover the nature, activity and destiny of the world. Its prince or ruler is the devil (John 12:31, 16: 11). Indeed, 'the whole world is in the power of the evil one' (1 John 5:19). It is in process of passing away (1 John 2:17), but while it lasts its antagonism to the Church, to God's people, is deep and bitter (e.g., 1 John 3:13). So these verses at the end of John 15, which we are considering, are embedded in a context of the hostility and hatred of the world, and they can only be understood in this context. 'If the world hates you,' Jesus has just been saying, 'know that it has hated me before it hated you. . . . If they persecuted me, they will persecute you. . . . It is to fulfil the word that is written in their law, "They hated me without a cause"' (John 15:18, 20, 25). Then, after our text, He goes on again: '. . . they will put you out of the synagogues; indeed, the hour is coming when whoever kills you will think that he is offering service to God. . .', and so on (John 16:1-4). The world hates, the world persecutes, the world ostracizes, the world kills. This is the antagonism of the world.

'But,' Jesus goes on (a mighty adversative conjunction!), 'But, when the Comforter is come. . . . He shall testify of me and ye also shall bear witness.' How is the Christian to react when faced with the opposition of the world? He is certainly not to retaliate. Nor is he to lick his wounds in self-pity. Nor is he to withdraw into safe and sheltered seclusion away from the disagreeable enmity of the world. No, he is bravely to bear witness to Jesus Christ before the world in the power of the Holy Spirit. Here is the world — sometimes indifferent and apathetic on the surface but underneath actively aggressive and rebellious. How are they to hear, to understand, to repeat and to believe? How are they to be brought to give sentence in favour of the Jesus who stands on trial before them? The answer is:

through our testimony. It is because of the unbelieving world's opposition to Christ that the Church's witness to Christ is needed.

The Son

Secondly, Christian witness is borne to the Son. 'When the Comforter is come, . . . he shall testify *of me*.' The world's hatred is focused upon Christ. 'They hated me without a cause.' 'If the world hates you, know that it has hated me before it hated you.' Therefore it is to Christ that the witness of the Spirit and the Church is borne. It is He who is on trial; it is for Him that the witness must speak.

So throughout the New Testament the gospel is fundamentally 'testimony to Jesus'. It is so called throughout the Apocalypse. John the seer describes himself in his introduction as God's servant 'who bore witness to the word of God and to the testimony of Jesus Christ' (Rev. 1:2). Similarly, the persecuted Church in the wilderness is described as 'those who keep the commandments of God and bear testimony to Jesus' (Rev. 12:17). It is also this witness to Christ which forms the uniting link between the Old and New Testaments, because, he comments, 'the testimony of Jesus is the spirit of prophecy' (Rev. 19:10).

Certainly the apostles were in no doubt about the direction of their witness. Jesus had told them both before and after His death and resurrection that they were to testify to Him (John 15:26, 27; Acts 1:8), and they obeyed His commission. Their sermons were full of Christ. They spoke of His life and ministry, 'how He went about doing good and healing all that were oppressed by the devil, for God was with Him', and they could thus speak because, they said, 'we are witnesses to all that He did both in the country of the Jews and in Jerusalem' (Acts 10:38, 39). They spoke also of His death, how 'men put Him to death by hanging Him on a tree' (Acts 10:39). There was no doubt about this as they were themselves witnesses 'of the sufferings of

Christ' (1 Pet. 5:1). Nor was it only the historical fact
of His death to which they testified, but its atoning significance. As Paul wrote to Timothy: the 'one mediator between
God and men, the man Christ Jesus . . . gave Himself as a ran-
som for all, the testimony to which was borne at the proper
time' (1 Tim. 2:5, 6). But, above all in the earliest days,
they bore witness to His resurrection. 'This Jesus God
raised up, and of that we all are witnesses', cried Peter in his
sermon on the Day of Pentecost (Acts 2:32). Again, in his
second sermon, 'You . . . killed the Author of life, whom
God raised from the dead. To this we are witnesses' (Acts
3:15; cf. also Acts 10:40, 41, 13:30, 31). It is not surprising
that Luke, in one of his summary verses in the Acts, thus
portrays the earliest preachers: 'with great power the
apostles gave their testimony to the resurrection of the Lord
Jesus' (Acts 4:33).

So much so-called 'testimony' today is really autobiography
and even sometimes thinly disguised self-advertisement, that
we need to regain a proper biblical perspective. All true
testimony is testimony to Jesus Christ, as He stands on trial
before the world.

The Father

Thirdly, Christian witness (which is witness to Christ before
the world) is borne by the Father. The Father is the chief
witness. Although it is the Spirit, Jesus said, who 'shall
testify of me', He emphasizes by a solemn repetition of
words that it is ultimately 'from the Father' that the Spirit
would come to bear witness. Jesus would send the Spirit
'*from the Father*, even the Spirit of truth, which proceedeth
from the Father.' Both the Holy Spirit's eternal Being in
heaven and His temporal mission on earth are from the Father.
He proceeds from the Father eternally. He came from the
Father historically. So, although the witness to Christ is
borne by the Spirit, as we shall see, it originated with the
Father.

It was and is the Father's supreme concern to honour and glorify the Son. 'It is my Father who glorifies me', said Jesus, and later boldly prayed: 'Father . . . glorify thy Son . . .' (John 8:54, 17:1). And it is in order that glory shall be brought to the Son by men, that the Father bears witness to Him. To grasp our Lord's understanding of this truth, it is necessary to look carefully at His words as recorded in John 5:30-41. Let me quote extracts from them: 'If I bear witness to myself, my testimony is not true (v. 31); there is another who bears witness to me, and I know that the testimony which he bears to me is true (v. 32). You sent to John, and he has borne witness to the truth (v. 33). Not that the testimony which I receive is from man. . . (v. 34). But the testimony which I have is greater than that of John; for the works which the Father has granted me to accomplish, these very works which I am doing, bear me witness that the Father has sent me (v. 36). And the Father who sent me has himself borne witness to me . . . (v. 37). You search the scriptures . . . and it is they that bear witness to me . . .' (v. 39). In this very illuminating discourse Jesus indicates that there are three possibilities of valid testimony to Himself, namely, His own self-testimony, testimony from man — represented by John the Baptist — and the testimony of the Father. He rejects the first two as insufficient (vv. 31, 34) and asserts that the greatest testimony which can be conceived has in fact been borne to Him, namely, that by the Father Himself. 'I know that the testimony which he bears to me', Jesus adds 'is true' (v. 32).

But the question may be asked, 'How did the Father bear witness to the Son? In what did His testimony consist?' Jesus does not leave us in doubt about the answer. First, it was written in the Old Testament Scriptures. Secondly, it could be heard and seen in the Son's historical words and works. The first part of the Father's testimony to the Son is the Old Testament Scripture. 'The scriptures', said Jesus '. . . bear witness to me' (v. 39). 'Moses . . . wrote of me'

(v. 46). This truth Jesus confirmed after the resurrection when, speaking with two disciples on the road to Emmaus, 'beginning with Moses and all the prophets, he interpreted to them in all the scriptures the things concerning himself' (Lk. 24:27). This, then, is the chief character and purpose of the Old Testament Scriptures. They are divine testimony to the coming Messiah of the Jews and Saviour of the world. It was by 'the Spirit of Christ' Himself within the prophets that they predicted 'the sufferings of Christ and the subsequent glory' (1 Pet. 1:10, 11).

The second part of the Father's testimony to the Son was in the very words which His contemporaries heard Him speak and in the very works they saw Him do. His words and works were not self testimony, because, rightly understood, they were not His words and works but the Father's who spoke and acted through Him. The works of Jesus were works which the Father granted Him to accomplish (v. 36) (cf. John 10:25). It was the same with His words. 'My teaching is not mine', He said 'but His who sent me' (John 7:16; cf. 12:49). He did not speak from Himself, on His own author-ity, but from God.[1] Putting the two together, Jesus could say: 'Do you not believe that I am in the Father and the Father in me? The words that I say to you I do not speak on my own authority; but the Father who dwells in me does His works. Believe me that I am in the Father and the Father in me; or else believe me for the sake of the works themselves' (John 14:10, 11). So the mighty works of the Messiah, 'signs' through which He manifested forth His glory (see John 2:11) and clear evidence that the Kingdom had come upon that very generation (see Mt. 12:28; Lk. 11:20), together with 'the gracious words which proceeded out of his mouth' (Lk. 4:22), owed their origin to the power of the Father who dwelt in Him and were thus the Father's testimony to Him.

Since these words and works of Jesus are now recorded

---

1. See the contrast in John 7:11 between *ek tou Theou* (from God) and *ap' emautou* (from myself).

and interpreted in the New Testament, we may say that the Father's testimony to the Son is now enshrined in the Scriptures of the Old and New Testaments. The written Word bears testimony to the Living Word. 'It was a favourite dictum of the preachers of a bygone day', Professor James Stewart has written, 'that, just as from every village in Britain there was a road which, linking on to other roads, would bring you to London at last, so from every text in the Bible, even the remotest and least likely, there was a road to Christ.'[2] To change the metaphor, Bible reading is like an old-fashioned treasure hunt. Every verse is a clue, which, leading to other clues, will guide you unerringly to the hidden treasure at last. Truly, 'the spirit of prophecy', whether in prophets of the Old Testament or apostles of the New, is 'the testimony of Jesus' (Rev. 19:10). If, then, we would bear witness to Jesus we shall be found constantly with the Bible in our hand, for it is there that the Father's testimony to the Son is to be found.

The Spirit

Fourthly Christian witness is borne (by the Father to the Son before the world) through the Holy Spirit. We must not imagine that the divine testimony borne to Christ before men is a dead testimony in the Scripture. It is made living through the Spirit. It is the Spirit who speaks to men in and through the Scripture. The Father's testimony is neither through the Scripture alone, nor through the Spirit alone, but through both. It is only when we assimilate this marvellous Trinitarian progression, the Father testifying to the Son through the Spirit, that we have begun to understand the biblical view of Christian witness.

Returning to our text, Jesus plainly declares that it is the Spirit, proceeding eternally and coming historically from the Father, who will bear witness to Him (v. 26). The Holy

2. James S. Stewart, *Heralds of God* (London: Hodder & Stoughton, 1946), p. 61.

Spirit is the executive of the Godhead. What God does in the world today, He accomplishes through the instrumentality of the Spirit. One of the Holy Spirit's chief tasks is to make Christ known to men, and Jesus reveals here how wonderfully competent He is for this work. Three truths are taught about Him.

First, He is the *Paraklētos*. Whether we translate this word 'Comforter' with the A.V. or 'Counselor' with the R.S.V., it is important to observe that, like 'witness', it is a legal word. Meaning, literally, 'called alongside' whether for help, comfort or advice, it came to be used of the barrister, the advocate, the counsel for the defence in a trial. Apart from these verses in the Upper Room Discourse in which the Holy Spirit is named the *Paraklētos*, the word only occurs elsewhere in 1 John 2:1, where it is written: 'We have an advocate with the Father, Jesus Christ the righteous'. So Jesus Christ is our advocate in heaven, while the Holy Spirit's advocacy is on earth. But whose advocate is the Holy Spirit on earth? Whose cause does He plead? To me the context demands only one answer, and that is, Christ's. The word may well be used in this discourse with other shades of meaning, and the Holy Spirit is certainly the Helper and Comforter of men, but the word's association with 'witnessing' in John 15:26, 27 and with 'convicting' in 16:8, which are both legal expressions, suggests strongly that it is the cause of Jesus Christ which the Holy Spirit is pleading. As Christ is our Advocate before the Father in heaven, so the Spirit is Christ's Advocate before the world on earth. We are but witnesses in court; the chief responsibility for the defence lies with God the Holy Spirit Himself.

Secondly, the Holy Spirit is called here 'the Spirit of truth'. 'When the Comforter is come . . ., even the Spirit of truth'. It is not only that truth characterizes Him; His very nature is truth. Thus, John writes in his First Epistle, 'The Spirit is the witness, because the Spirit is the truth' (1 John 5:7). That He should prove a false witness is unthinkable. His witness is always true, because He is true.

The Holy Spirit's third qualification to bear witness to Christ is that He is the Spirit of Christ. He is called in the New Testament almost indiscriminately 'the Spirit of God' and 'the Spirit of Christ', because He proceeds eternally from the Father and the Son. And in the verses we are studying at the end of John 15, Jesus says of Him: 'whom I shall send to you from the Father' (cf. Acts 2:33).

If the Holy Spirit is both Paraclete and Spirit of truth and Spirit of Christ, we can indeed understand that Jesus goes on to say: 'He will bear witness to me'. He is perfectly and uniquely qualified to do so. The purpose of His coming was to make Christ known, 'glorifying' Him to the Church (John 16:14) and 'testifying' to Him before the world (John 15:26).[3]

The Church

This brings us at last to the fifth aspect of Christian witness, which concerns the preacher. We have been a long time reaching this point, but it is only now that we shall be able to see the preacher's work in perspective. We may summarize the biblical view of Christian witness by saying that it is *borne before the world by the Father to the Son through the Spirit and the Church*. If the Father's living testimony to the Son is borne through the Spirit, it is through the Church also. So Jesus says: 'The Spirit of truth . . . shall testify of me and ye also shall bear witness'. Peter made a similar statement in one of his sermons before the Sanhedrin, when he said: 'We are witnesses to these things, and so is the Holy Spirit . . .' (Acts 5:32; cf. 1:8).

This double witness of the Spirit and the Church is a very interesting phenomenon. It is an example of the fact that valid witness must always be plural. The evidence of a single witness was insufficient in the Old Testament for any charge to be substantiated. 'A single witness shall not pre-

3. For the Spirit's inner witness to the believer, which is a different subject, see, e.g., Rom. 8:16; 1 John 5:10.

vail against a man for any crime or for any wrong in connection with any offence that he has committed; only on the evidence of two witnesses, or of three witnesses, shall a charge be sustained' (Deut. 19:15; cf. 17:6, 7; Num. 35:30; Heb. 10:28). This principle was carried into the New Testament. Jesus told us quite plainly that if a brother who has sinned against us will not listen when we face him with his fault alone, we are to 'take one or two others' along with us 'that every word may be confirmed by the evidence of two or three witnesses' (Mt. 18:15, 16; cf. 2 Cor. 13:1, 1 Tim. 5:19). Moreover, this principle holds not only in witnessing against somebody's misdeeds, but also when witnessing to the truth. Is this not why Jesus sent out the Twelve and the Seventy 'two by two' (Mk. 6:7; Lk. 10:1). It is certainly the explicit reason why He claimed the Father's testimony to Him as corroborating His own self-testimony. 'In your law', He said 'it is written that the testimony of two men is true; I bear witness to myself, and the Father who sent me bears witness to me' (John 8:17, 18). Perhaps this throws light also on the identity of the 'two witnesses' in the Revelation who were given 'power to prophesy' for a certain period (Rev. 11:3-17). All this shows the value of corporate witness, of the immense possibilities of a whole local congregation united in witness concerning Jesus Christ to the parish or neighbourhood in which the church is situated. If by the evidence of only two or three witnesses every word is confirmed and established, who can resist the impact of a total witnessing Church?

Experience

Important, however, as united congregational witness is, the preacher has a particular role to testify to Jesus Christ. For the adequate fulfilment of his duty, he will need two special qualifications, experience and humility. We shall consider each in turn.

By 'experience' I do not now mean experience of the preaching ministry or experience of life in general, necessary as these are to the preacher. I mean rather a personal experience of Jesus Christ Himself. This is the first and indispensable mark of the Christian witness. He cannot speak from hearsay. He would not be a 'witness' if he did. He must be able to speak from his own personal experience.

This should be quite plain from the legal associations of the word. One of the ways in which it is used is in the ratification of legal transactions. For instance when Jeremiah bought a field at Anathoth from his cousin, he wrote about it: 'I signed the deed, sealed it, got witnesses, and weighed the money on scales', and he laid great stress on the fact that the deed of purchase was first signed and sealed, and then given to Baruch, 'in the presence of the witnesses' (Jer. 32: 9-12, cf. vv. 25 and 44). Similarly, in the public place within the gate, with the elders of the city as witnesses, Boaz bought both a field from Naomi and Ruth the Moabitess to be his wife (Ruth 4:1-12).[4] These witnesses are so called because they 'witnessed' an agreement. They heard with their own ears the undertaking of the contracting parties. They saw with their own eyes the signing and sealing of the deed. Perhaps this is clearest of all when God Himself is called upon as witness. One example from the Old Testament will suffice. Jeremiah ends his letter to the exiles in Babylon with the solemn words 'I am the one who knows, and I am witness, says the Lord' (Jer. 29:23)[5]. God is the best witness of all because He knows all things. His eyes are in every place. No secret can be concealed from Him. It is for this reason that the apostle Paul four times in his Epistles, when he is asserting some personal truth about his hidden motives or private actions, solemnly cries out 'God is my witness' (Rom. 1:9; 2 Cor. 1:23; Phil. 1:8; 1 Thess. 2:5). Only God could read his thoughts. Only God knew whether his motives were sincere and whether his heart was clean. So when he

4. For the use of stones instead of people as witnesses to a covenant cf. Gn. 31:43-50 and Josh. 24:22, 25.

5. Other examples are Judg. 11:10; 1 Sam. 12:5; Job 16:19; Jer. 42:5; Mi. 1:2; Mal. 2:14, 3:5.

was accused or suspected by men, he could call upon none but God as his witness.

The other juridical use of the word 'witness' belongs to courts of law. A citizen who appears in court as a witness in a prosecution for dangerous driving must have seen the accident take place and can therefore give evidence. The Greek verb *marturasthai* or *marturein* means, according to the Grimm-Thayer lexicon 'to be a witness, to bear witness, testify, i.e. to affirm that one has seen or heard or experienced something'.[6] Here is another definition: 'The witness is he who has a direct knowledge of certain facts and declares before a court of justice what he has seen or heard. He bears witness to what he knows'.[7]

These ideas in the legal use of the word 'witness' are carried over in the Bible into the sphere of Christian witness. Referring again to the text which is the basis of this chapter, Jesus said to His disciples not only 'ye also shall bear witness', but He remarked upon their fitness for this ministry in the words 'because ye have been with me from the beginning (John 15:27). They could bear witness *to* Him, because they had been *with* Him. This was their essential qualification. If they had not known Him, they could not have testified to Him. Since they had known Him, they must.[8] He repeats the same sequence after the resurrection when He says to them first 'You are witnesses of these things' (Lk. 24:48) and then 'You shall be my witnesses' (Acts 1:8; cf. also 1:21, 22, 2:32, 3:15, 4:33, etc.). In order to *bear* witness, one must *be* a witness.

This qualification is so important, and receives such reiterated emphasis in the New Testament, that we must enlarge on it a little further. The commonest coupling is between the

6. *A Greek-English Lexicon of the New Testament*, 2d ed. rev. (Edinburgh: T. & T. Clark, 1892), p. 390.
7. S. de Diètrich in J.-J. von Allmen's *Vocabulary of the Bible*, article "Witness."
8. The sin of failing to testify when one has been a witness is condemned in Lev. 5:1.

verbs to 'see' and to 'testify'. The best witness is the eye-witness.[9] John the Baptist had this qualification. It is written of him: 'John bore witness "I saw the Spirit descend as a dove from heaven, and it remained on him. . . . I have seen and have borne witness that this is the Son of God"' (John 1:32, 34). Jesus Christ Himself advanced the same claim to personal knowledge and sight, when to Nicodemus He said: 'We speak of what we know, and bear witness to what we have seen' (John 3:11-13).[10] Next, we may mention St. John who uses the categories of seeing and witnessing more frequently than the other New Testament writers. The preface to his first epistle includes the well-known words 'the life was made manifest, and we saw it, and testify to it', and later, 'we have seen and testify that the Father hath sent His Son as the Saviour of the world' (1 John 1:2, 4:14; cf. John 19:35). Our last example is the apostle Paul to whom after his conversion Ananias said, 'The God of our fathers appointed you to know His will, to see the Just One, and to hear a voice from His mouth; for you will be a witness for Him to all men of what you have seen and heard' (Acts 22:15, cf. 23:11, 26:22).

I make no apology for this catalogue of examples. We need to be convinced by this cumulative evidence that the biblical idea of Christian witness presupposes a firsthand, living experience of the salvation of Jesus Christ. The apostles saw and heard the historical Jesus objectively. But the words of the risen Jesus to St. Paul already suggest the propriety of extending the notion of witness to a subjective and mystical experience of Christ, for He said to Paul: 'I have appeared to you for this purpose, to appoint you to serve and bear witness to the things in which you have seen me and to those in which I will appear to you' (Acts 26:16).

9. See, however, Lk. 14:22 for testimony to what has been *heard;* John 2:25, Acts 15:8, 25:6 for testimony to what is *known;* and 3 John 3, 6 for testimony to one's general experience of a person.

10. Cf. 3:32, and also 1 Tim. 6:12, 13 and Rev. 1:5, 3:14, where the 'good confession' and 'faithful witness' of Jesus are mentioned.

There is no reason to suppose that these future experiences of Christ were objective appearances such as he says the Damascus Road revelation was. Rather were they inward and spiritual, and to these too he must bear witness. So must we.

In our preaching, we do not just expound words which have been committed to our stewardship. Nor do we only proclaim as heralds a mighty deed of redemption which has been done But, in addition, we expound these words and proclaim this deed as witnesses, as those who have come to a vital experience of this Word and Deed of God. We have heard His still, small voice through His Word. We have seen His redeeming Deed as having been done for us, and we have entered by faith into the immeasurable benefits of it. Our task is not to lecture about Jesus with philosophical detachment. We have become personally involved in Him. His revelation and redemption have changed our lives. Our eyes have been opened to see Him, and our ears unstopped to hear Him, as our Saviour and our Lord. We *are* witnesses; so we must *bear* witness. Certainly, we shall teach men systematically about Him, and we shall boldly herald the good news of what He has accomplished by His death. But we shall not fail to commend Him to our hearers out of our own personal experience. 'It is quite futile,' said William Temple, 'saying to people "Go to the cross". We must be able to say "Come to the cross". And there are only two voices which can issue that invitation with effect. One is the voice of the Sinless Redeemer, with which we cannot speak; the other is the voice of the forgiven sinner, who knows himself forgiven. That is our part.'

If the governing idea of witness is that of personal experience, it goes without saying that there must be an exact correspondence between our experience and our testimony. We must be strictly honest. The Bible warns us of the serious sin of false witness. The ninth commandment categorically forbids us to bear false witness against our neighbor, (Ex. 20:16; Dt. 5:20; cf. Ex. 23:1) and so mean was the false witness considered to be that the magistrates were instructed to 'do to him as he had meant to do to his brother (Dt. 19:16-21). The horror with which this sin was regarded may be judged from the fact that 'a false witness who breathes out lies' is listed in the Book of Proverbs as one of the six things which God hates (Prov. 6:19), while Jesus included it in His list of the vile things which proceed out of the evil human heart (Mt. 15:19).[11]

This, then, is the alternative before us. Our witness may be 'false' or 'faithful'. 'A faithful witness does not lie, but a false witness breathes out lies' (Prov. 14:5, cf. v. 25) The devil is the chief false witness. He is a slanderer, the accuser of the brethren, 'a liar and the father of lies' (Rev. 12:10; John 8:44). But the Christian preacher must be an unimpeachably true witness. It is not just that we must take great pains to be accurate in our exposition of the Word of God,[12] but that we must neither overstate nor understate the facts of our own experience. If it is required in stewards that a man be found faithful, it is required in witnesses also. The faithfulness of a steward consists in his dispensing to the household exactly what has been committed to him; the faithfulness of a witness lies in his declaring with honesty and candour exactly what he knows, neither concealing part of the truth, nor distorting it, nor embellishing it. It is so easy to exaggerate, to give to others the impression that we have progressed further along the narrow way than we really have. We must have the honesty to confess the truth. We should not be afraid to say with the apostle, 'not as though I had already attained, either were already perfect' (Phil.

11. For other references to 'false witness' see Ps. 27:12, 35:11; Prov. 12: 17, 19:5, 9, 24:18; Mk. 14:55-63; Acts 6:13, 7:58.
12. Paul gives a hypothetical example of this in 1 Cor. 15:15, where he says that if Christ has not been raised from the dead, the apostles are false witnesses of God, since they have consistently testified to His resurrection.

3:12, A.V.). The true witness is devoid of any suspicion of hypocrisy; he is transparently sincere.

All this lays upon us who are called to be witnesses to Christ the solemn obligation to take heed to ourselves, and not to neglect the culture of our own soul, lest we become dumb witnesses and have nothing to say. Truly the apostles were right to give themselves to prayer and to the ministry of the Word, for preaching without prayer is an empty mockery. There is no greater need for the preacher than that he should know God. I care not about his lack of eloquence and artistry, about his ill-constructed discourse or his poorly enunciated message, if only it is evident that God is a reality to him and that he has learned to abide in Christ. The preparation of the heart is of far greater importance than the preparation of the sermon. The preacher's words, however clear and forceful, will not ring true unless he speaks from conviction born of experience. Many sermons which conform to all the best homiletical rules, yet have a hollow sound. There is something indefinably perfunctory about the preacher of such sermons. The matter of his sermon gives evidence of a well-stocked, well-disciplined mind; he has a good voice, a fine bearing, and restrained gestures; but somehow his heart is not in his message; it can not be said as a young clerk in a dry-goods store once said about Peter Marshall, 'He seems to know God, and he helps me to know Him better'.[13] Alexander Whyte apparently once said: 'Though you had the whole Bodleian Library and did not know yourself, you would not preach a sermon worth hearing'.[14] This is true, but more important even than to know oneself is to know God.

The preaching of a witness has a spontaneity about it, an infectious warmth, a simple directness, a depth of reality, which are all due to an intimate knowledge of God. So we

13. Catherine Marshall, *A Man Called Peter* (New York: McGraw-Hill, 1952), p. 43.
14. Quoted by Leslie J. Tizard in *Preaching — the Art of Communication* (London: George Allen & Unwin, 1958), p. 16.

must hunger and thirst after Him. We must claim the promise of Jesus that He will manifest Himself to those who love Him and who prove their love by their obedience (John 14:21). We shall remember that the real preparation of a sermon is not the few hours which are specifically devoted to it, but the whole stream of the preacher's Christian experience thus far, of which the sermon is a distilled drop. As E. M. Bounds has put it, 'The man, the whole man, lies behind the sermon. Preaching is not the performance of an hour. It is the outflow of a life. It takes twenty years to make a sermon, because it takes twenty years to make a man'.[15]

It is surely because such an experience of God, as we have been describing, is more precious than life itself that witness in the New Testament is closely associated with suffering, and that the Greek word for a witness (*martus*) gradually came to mean a martyr (see Acts 22:20 and Rev. 1:9, 2:13, 6:9, 12:11, 17:6, 20:4). May God give us more men of such calibre today whose knowledge of Jesus Christ is of such surpassing worth that they are prepared to suffer for their testimony to Him and, if need be, seal their testimony with their blood.

Humility

If experience is one indispensable mark of the true Christian witness, humility is the other. Every preacher knows the insidious temptation to vainglory to which the pulpit exposes him. We stand there in a prominent position, lifted above the congregation, the focus of their gaze and the object of their attention. It is a perilous position indeed. But I venture to say that a proper understanding of the nature and purpose of Christian witness will be a helpful safeguard against the dangers of pride. Let us remember that Christian witness is witness *to Christ*. It is not self-testimony; and if

15. E. M. Bounds, *Power through Prayer* (London: Marshall Brothers), p. 11.

we do speak from our own experience, it is only to exemplify
our teaching about Christ. John the Baptist may in this
respect be regarded as the perfect illustration of the witness.
It is written of him, 'He came for testimony, to bear witness
to the light. . . . He was not the light, but came to bear
witness to the light' (John 1:7, 8, cf. vv. 15, 19). And when
he had done his work, and as a result of his witness his
disciples began one by one to leave his side and follow
Jesus (e.g., John 1:35-42), he seems to have felt no resent-
ment, but only pleasure in the fulfilment of his task. He was
like a forerunner or outrider, who goes on in advance to prepare the people for the coming of the king. But when the
king comes, who pays any attention to the fore-runner?
Again, in another metaphor he used, Jesus is the Heavenly
Bridegroom who has come to fetch His Bride. John is 'the
friend of the bridegroom', whose duty has been to make
arrangements for the marriage. But now the Bridegroom
has come, you would not expect the Bride to have thoughts
for any but her groom. The 'friend of the bridegroom' has
no wish to come between the Bride and her Bridegroom.
He has accomplished his task. The Bridegroom now 'has
the Bride.' The 'friend of the bridegroom' retires into the
background and 'rejoices greatly at the bridegroom's voice.'
'This joy of mine,' adds John, 'is now full', and he concludes
with a perfect summary of the attitude of a humble witness:
'He must increase, but I must decrease' (John 3:25-30). We
do not want to draw the attention of people to ourselves, or
to come between them and Christ. The overriding purpose
of our witness-ministry is that they will see Christ and
give their allegiance to Him.

In the church in which I serve in London a famous picture
hangs on the east wall behind the Communion Table. It
measures about 12 feet by 9 and dominates the interior of
the church. It was painted by William Westall and was
presented by King George IV when the church was consecrated in 1824. It depicts the Lord Jesus, manacled but
majestic, surrounded by evil-looking priests and coarse soldiers

who mock at Him. All round His head are the hands of these men, pointing to the object of their derision. I see in this picture a symbol of our ministry. Jesus Christ is the centre of our message. We are but signposts pointing to Him. What those soldiers and priests in the picture do in scorn and hatred we do in love and worship. And the more our vision is filled with Him, the less shall we lapse into self-centred vanity.

But Christian witness is not just witness to Christ. It is also, and fundamentally, a witness borne to Him by the Father through the Spirit. I do not mean to imply that our human witness is either unnecessary or unimportant. But on the other hand, let us see it in perspective, and we shall then be less inclined to conceit. Witness to Jesus Christ before the world does not finally depend on us; it is a mighty testimony initiated by the Father and continued through the Spirit. And if the Spirit uses the Church as the means through which His witness is chiefly exercised, the credit is due to the Spirit not the Church.

In this humble position of witnesses, having some small share in the Father's testimony to the Son through the Spirit, may we always rejoice to be.

CHAPTER FOUR

A FATHER

The Preacher's Love and Gentleness

To THINK and speak of the preacher as a 'father' may at first sound somewhat strange. The ideas conveyed by the title do not, strictly speaking, belong to the field of homiletics at all. But St. Paul did not hesitate to call himself the 'father' of the Corinthians, the Galatians and the Thessalonians, as well as of certain individuals, and there is no doubt that a father's qualities, particularly of gentleness and love, which the Apostle mentions, are indispensable to the preacher as portrayed in the New Testament.

There is such a rich variety of biblical metaphors to illustrate the preaching ministry that they overlap one another to some extent, and it is not easy to reconcile them. For example, if the 'steward' brought us in imagination into a house, the 'herald' into a public place in the city, and the 'witness' into the law courts, the 'father' brings us back into the house again. However, the father's relation to his children is, of course, quite different from the steward's to the household. It is one of affection rather than duty, and what is new in the 'father' metaphor should now be apparent. In order to distinguish it clearly, it will be helpful to contrast the particular responsibilities of these various men and their offices. The steward's responsibility is really to the goods entrusted to him. That is, the preacher must be faithful in the message he dispenses to the household. The responsibility of the Christian herald is to proclaim God's mighty deed of redemption through Christ, and to appeal to men to respond to it. The witness must enjoy a firsthand experience of that to which he testifies. Thus far, the preacher is preoccupied with his message, what it is and how he delivers it, and with himself, his personal experience of what he is preaching. But in the 'father' metaphor the preacher becomes concerned about his family, about the people to whom he is ministering the word, and about his relationship to them.

Preaching involves a personal relationship between preacher and congregation. The preacher is not like an actor who declaims from the stage, while the audience remain spectators. Nor is he only a herald, shouting his proclamation from the housetops, as it were, a middleman between king and people, while the people remain unknown to him and he to them. He is a father to his children. A loving family relationship exists between them. They belong to each other. And before, during and after the sermon the preacher is, or should be, conscious of this relationship in which he is involved. This may not be so obvious in evangelistic preaching in the open air or in a campaign, when most of the people are strangers to the preacher. But it is evident to the preacher who has the inestimable privilege of ministering to a settled congregation. Such a preacher can never forget that he is a pastor as well. As Bishop Phillips Brooks said, 'The preacher needs to be pastor, that he may preach to real men. The pastor must be preacher, that he may keep the dignity of his work alive. The preacher, who is not a pastor, grows remote. The pastor, who is not a preacher, grows petty.'[1] He will find that his sermons to some extent express, and are determined by, the relationship which he enjoys with his people. He is their father; they his children.

The picture is slightly complicated by the fact that the average preacher may be said to have two separate congregations, those within the family and those without. The herald makes his public proclamation to all and sundry, and the witness gives evidence for Jesus Christ who stands on trial before the world. These metaphors illustrate evange-

1. Phillips Brooks, *Lectures on Preaching*. (1877), (London: H. R. Allenson, 1895), p. 77.

listic preaching. The steward, however, takes care of the household, and the father of his family. Nevertheless, I believe the qualities of a father are to be displayed in the preacher, whoever the people are to whom he happens to be speaking, whether insiders, outsiders, or nominal adherents to the Church.

A Father's Authority Forbidden

In what sense, then, may the preacher be called a 'father'? The word is so closely associated with priests of the Church of Rome that we may have strongly entrenched Protestant prejudices to be overcome before we are receptive to the idea! The subject is an interesting example of the need for caution in biblical interpretation, for we find in the New Testament three uses of the simile 'father', two legitimate and one illegitimate. Taking the illegitimate use first, we are familiar with the words of Jesus to His disciples: 'Call no man your father on earth, for you have one Father, who is in heaven (Mt. 23:9). In the context Jesus is warning His followers of the pride and hypocrisy of the Pharisees, who thirsted after status, who loved 'the place of honour at feasts and the best seats in the synagogues, and salutations in the market places, and being called rabbi by men' (Mt. 23:6, 7). The Pharisees loved to be given deferential titles. It flattered them. It gave them a sense of superiority over other people. In contrast to them, Jesus said that there were three titles His disciples were not to assume or be given, 'Rabbi' (that is, teacher), 'father' and 'master'. We are principally concerned now with the designation 'father'. What did Jesus mean by it?

The father exercises authority over his children by reason of the fact that they depend upon him. I suggest that what Jesus is saying is that we are never to adopt towards a fellow man in the Church the attitude of dependence which a child has towards his father, nor are we to require others to be or become spiritually dependent on us. That this is what Jesus intended is confirmed by the reason He gives, namely, 'for you have one Father, who is in heaven'. Spiritual dependence is due to God our Heavenly Father. He is our Creator, both physically and spiritually, and as creatures we depend utterly upon His grace. But we do not and must not depend on our fellow creatures. Our desire, as preachers, is (like St. Paul) to 'present every man mature in Christ' (Col. 1:28). We long to see the members of our congregation grow up into independent, adult, spiritual maturity in Christ, looking to Him for the supply of all their needs, since it is 'in Christ' that God 'has blessed us . . . with every spiritual blessing' (Eph. 1:3). We have no desire to keep our church members tied to our own apron strings and running round us like children round their mother. There are in every church some weak and feeble souls who love to fuss round the minister and are constantly seeking interviews with him to consult him about their spiritual problems. This should be resisted, and that strenuously. Gently but firmly we should make it clear that God's purpose is that His children should look to Him as their Father, and not to men. Perhaps I may suggest in passing that the reason for Christ's prohibition of the other two titles is substantially the same. We are 'not to be called rabbi', posing as an authoritative Teacher in our own right, nor 'master' as if we expected men to give us their slavish obedience. We are their slaves, not they ours (Mt. 23:11).

The principal explanation of our Lord's categorical refusal to allow this kind of thing in the Christian Church is that He saw in it an affront to God. God is our Father (Mt. 23:9), Christ is our Master (Mt. 23:10), and (although this is not explicitly stated in the text) the Holy Spirit is our teacher. To set ourselves up, therefore, as the fathers, masters and teachers of men, is to usurp the glory of the Eternal Trinity, and to arrogate to ourselves an authority over men which belongs to God alone. The second reason for our Lord's insistence on this point may be seen in His words 'and you are all brethren' (Mt. 23:8). Certainly, there are differences of office and ministry in the Christian Church, but these do not affect the basic equality of all Christian people. It is ridiculous for one Christian to claim the authority of a father over a fellow Christian and demand his subordination as a child if the two men are in reality brothers. The Pharisees loved to make the common people cowtow to them. Christian ministers are to do nothing of the sort.

A Father's Relationship and Affection

It is, then, the *authority* of a father over dependent children which is forbidden to us. But the 'father' metaphor is used in two other ways in the New Testament, which are permissible. Both occur at the end of 1 Corinthians 4, and I will quote from verse 14:

> 'I do not write this to make you ashamed, but to admonish you as my beloved children. For though you have countless guides in Christ, you do not have many fathers. For I became your father in Christ Jesus through the gospel. I urge you, then, be imitators of me. Therefore I sent to you Timothy, my beloved and faithful child in the Lord, to remind you of my ways in Christ, as I teach them everywhere in every church. . . . What do you wish? Shall I come to you with a rod, or with love in a spirit of gentleness?'

The first legitimate use of the father-child simile, which occurs in this passage, is in the case of one who has been the means of another's conversion. Paul does not hesitate to write to the Galatians: 'My little children, with whom I am again in travail until Christ be formed in you!' (Gal. 4:19). The metaphor here is a little confused. They are already his 'little children', but their very spiritual life seems in danger, so that he feels as if he must endure birth pangs on their behalf again. In this metaphor he is their mother. He gave birth to them when he visited their cities on his first missionary journey. Similarly, he speaks of having 'begotten' the Corinthians 'through the gospel' (1 Cor. 4:15,

A.V.),[2] referring no doubt to his missionary visit to Corinth during the second missionary journey. The Apostle spoke of the same relationship with individuals whom he had led to Christ. Onesimus, the runaway slave, had evidently been converted through Paul's ministry while he was a prisoner in Rome, so that the Apostle could write to Philemon: 'I appeal to you for my child, Onesimus, whose father I have become in my imprisonment' (Philem. 10). Since he calls both Timothy and Titus his children, it is likely that it was through him that they became Christians also.[3]

The second legitimate use of the 'father-child' metaphor is to convey an intimately affectionate relationship. This is the sense in 1 Corinthians 4, and it is in this way that I am using the metaphor as a description of what the preacher should be. The Corinthians were the Apostle's 'beloved children' (v. 14), and every preacher may come to think of the congregation he serves in the same way. In order to clarify what he means, Paul draws a distinction between the 'guide' and the 'father'. The word in verse 15, which is translated by the R.S.V. 'guides' and by the A.V. 'instructors', is *paidagōgous*. The *paidagōgos* was the tutor of a child during his minority.[4] He was normally a slave, but he had to supervise his ward's behaviour, including his dress and food, his speech and manners. He was not the child's instructor (for he did little if any teaching), but his disciplinarian. He is usually portrayed in ancient drawings with a whip in his hand, as he was allowed to administer corporal punishment. This is why the Apostle writes in verse 21, 'Shall I come to you with a rod?' or, as Bishop J. W. C. Wand puts it, 'with a big stick'?[5] That is, did the Corinthians want Paul to be

2. The R.S.V. is 'I became your father in Christ Jesus through the gospel'.

3. For Timothy see 1 Cor. 4:17; 1 Tim. 1:2; 2 Tim. 1:2, 2:1. For Titus see Tit. 1:4. Cf. also Peter's reference to Mark in 1 Pet. 5:13 and John's reference throughout his first epistle to his 'little children'.

4. Cf. Paul's argument in Gal. 3:23 — 4:7, where the law is our *paidagogos* to bring us to Christ.

their *paidagōgos*, to treat them with severity and to chastise them? Surely not! 'You have countless guides in Christ,' he says, but 'you do not have many fathers' (1 Cor. 4:15). In other words, there were plenty of people ready to discipline them, but not many to love them with a father's love, which is what Paul did and wanted to continued to do.

It is plain, however, from this passage that the father may sometimes have to play the part of the *paidagōgos*. It is true of every father that he 'disciplines him whom he loves, and chastises every son whom he receives' (Heb. 12:6 from Prov. 3:12). And the minister is endowed with a certain authority for discipline. Such authority is no more inconsistent with charity than it is with humility. Such a combination of attitudes is interestingly exemplified in 1 Thessalonians 2, where in one verse St. Paul indicates his apostolic authority by claiming that his word was not 'the word of men' but 'the word of God', and in another verse reminds his readers of his behaviour towards them, saying: 'You know how, like a father with his children, we exhorted each one of you and encouraged you and charged you to lead a life worthy of God . . .' (1 Thess. 2:13).

Love, then, is the chief quality of a father to which the Apostle refers when he uses the metaphor to illustrate his ministry; not a soft or sickly sentimentality, but a strong, unselfish love which cares and which is not incompatible with discipline. This love is the preeminent Christian virtue. Paul himself, the great apostle of grace and faith, writes that love is the firstfruit of the Spirit (Gal. 5:22). Champion of theological orthodoxy that he is, he even declares that love is superior to knowledge, since 'knowledge puffs up' while 'love builds up' (1 Cor. 8:1-3). And in his exquisite hymn to charity in 1 Cor. 13, he leaves us in no doubt about its indispensable necessity in the preacher: 'If I speak in the tongues of men and of angels, but have not love, I am a noisy gong

5. *The New Testament Letters* (Oxford: Oxford University Press, 1944), *loc. cit.*

or a clanging cymbal. And if I have prophetic powers, and understand all mysteries and all knowledge, and if I have all faith, so as to remove mountains, but have not love, I am nothing' (1 Cor. 13:1-2). He could not have made his point more emphatically. The loveless preacher is not only discordant noise. He is worse and less than that. He is 'nothing'.

Having sought to show that when the Apostle uses the 'father' metaphor he is thinking not so much of a father's authority as of a father's affection, we are now in a position to ask in what ways we may expect this love to manifest itself and, in particular, how it is likely to express itself in the preaching ministry. I have six suggestions to make.

A Father's Understanding

First, a father's love will make us understanding in our approach. The people of the congregation to whom we preach have many problems, intellectual, moral, personal, domestic. Peter Marshall once advised men in Gettysburg Theological Seminary: 'You must root your preaching in reality, remembering that the people before you have problems — doubts, fears and anxieties gnawing at their faith. Your problem and mine is to get behind the conventional fronts that sit row upon row in the pews. . . .'[6] He was surely quite right. Too much of our preaching is academic and theoretical; we need to bring it down into the practical realities of everyday life. It is not enough to give an accurate exposition of some passage of the Word of God if we do not relate it to the actual needs of men. This is the fascination of preaching — applying God's word to man's need. The preacher should be as familiar with man in his world as he is with God.

But the question is how can we come to understand the problems which are perplexing and burdening the people we

6. Catherine Marshall, *A Man Called Peter* (New York: McGraw-Hill, 1952), p. 224.

serve?   The simple answer is: by love.   A father labours
to understand his children as they grow up.   He cares about
them so deeply that he will do his utmost to enter into their
hopes and fears, their weaknesses and their difficulties.   So
too a preacher, if he loves his people with a father's love,
will take time and trouble to discover what their problems
are.   The minister usually leads a sheltered life.   He may
know something about home life, but he has probably had
no experience of business life.   He has never had to face the
ethical decisions, the pressures, the competition, the relation-
ships with colleagues, the strain, the daily commuting, which
are the common lot of the average business man.   As likely
as not, the congregation are aware of this, and are quite convinced that their minister does not understand their difficulties.
He talks glibly about the Christian life and Christian witness.
But has he ever had to stand alone as a Christian in an office
or store or factory with no fellowship with other Christians?
It really is of the greatest importance that we think ourselves
into the situation in which our people find themselves; that
we identify ourselves with them in their sorrows, responsibilities and perplexities; and that we do not live, or appear to
them to live, in a remote ivory tower.   Such an estrangement
between preacher and congregation is most harmful both to
the proclamation and to the reception of the message.   Speaker
and hearers are not on the same wave length.

How can we effect a rapprochement?   For one thing, we
shall have to read some books, magazines and newspapers,
not only to deepen our knowledge of human nature in
general, but in particular to get to know how people live
and think.   And we shall let people talk to us.   There is
no quicker way of bridging the gulf between preacher and
people than meeting them in their homes and in our home.
The effective preacher is always a diligent pastor.   Only if
he makes time each week both for visiting people and for
interviewing them, will he be *en rapport* with them as he
preaches.   The more they speak to him in his study on

weekdays, the better he will speak to them from the pulpit on Sundays.

Love will help the preacher to be understanding in his approach not only because he will then take trouble to get to know his people and their problems, but also because he will be the better able to appreciate them when he knows them. Love has a strange intuitive faculty. Jesus our Lord possessed it to perfection. Again and again it is said of Him that He knew people's thoughts. Indeed, St. John writes, 'He knew all men and needed no one to bear witness of man; for He Himself knew what was in man (John 2:25). Men felt instinctively that He understood them. He is the great *kardiognōstes* (Acts 1:24), or heart-knower, who 'searches mind and heart' (Rev. 2:23), and we should seek from Him insight to be and do the same. Love, the unselfish care which longs to understand and so to help, is one of the greatest secrets of communication. It is when the preacher loves his people that they are likely to say of him, 'He understands us'.

A Father's Gentleness

Secondly, a father's love will make us gentle in our manner. So many of us are naturally brusque and rough handed. By temperament we are neither meek nor sensitive. Yet the true father, whatever his character may be like and however strict a disciplinarian he may be, shows a certain tenderness towards his children. His love makes him gentle. This quality marked the character of the Lord Jesus. Did He not say of Himself 'I am gentle and lowly in heart' (Mt. 11:29), and did not Paul write of 'the meekness and gentleness of Christ'? (2 Cor. 10:1). In this too 'a disciple is not above his teacher; nor a servant above his master'. Indeed, 'it is enough for the disciple to be like the teacher, and the servant like his master' (Mt. 10:24, 25). So Paul expresses to the Corinthians his desire to come to them 'with love in a spirit of gentleness' (1 Cor. 4:21), the very 'gentleness' which is part of the fruit of the Spirit (Gal. 5:23). In all these places 'gentleness' is the same word, *prautēs*.

And if gentleness is to characterize all Christians as it characterized Christ, it is never more necessary or becoming than in preachers and teachers. A good shepherd will 'gently lead those that are with young' (Is. 40:11). Indeed, sometimes he will need to be so tender that he seems more like a nurse with her babies than a shepherd with his lambs. 'We were gentle among you,' wrote Paul to the Thessalonians, 'like a nurse taking care of her children' (1 Thess. 2:7). And how we need such gentleness! Children grow up slowly. It is foolish to expect them to have the wisdom and decorum of adults while they are still infants. We must be patient with them. They will sometimes seem dull of understanding and we shall be as exasperated with their obtuseness as Jesus was with the Twelve. But still we must persevere. We must never lose heart or temper, or give up in despair. We are called to keep watch over men's souls (Heb. 13:17); we must never relax our vigilance. And when we are sore tried, perhaps by factions in the church or the outbreak of false teaching, we must remember our instructions: 'The Lord's servant must not be quarrelsome, but kindly to everyone, an apt teacher, forbearing, correcting his opponents with gentleness' (2 Tim. 2:24, 25).

And here is another point: it is tragic to see a minister become sour. After long years of disappointment and frustration, with few visible results and little audible appreciation to cheer him on his way, the minister sometimes grows embittered. Then he turns to cruel sarcasm. But such sarcasm is not a weapon which love will ever use. It is often a crooked expression of self-pity and conceit. We are not respected or honoured or appreciated as we think we should be, so we take our revenge in sarcasm. It is a sure sign of self-love, for if we loved others more than we loved ourselves, we should never give vent to our bitterness at their expense. It is love that will keep us sweet. St. Paul concedes that he has had to say some harsh things about the arrogant complacency of the Corinthians, but he hastens to add that his purpose in doing so was not to humiliate them but to bring them to a better mind. 'I do not write this to make you ashamed, but to admonish you as my beloved children' (1 Cor. 4:14). A true parent will never want to score off his children, or make them feel small in public. He will love them too much for that. Children need encouragement often more than admonition, to have their good behaviour commended as much as their bad behaviour rebuked. Fathers are not to 'provoke' their children, 'lest they become discouraged' (Col. 3:21, cf. Eph. 6:4). 'I have been greatly impressed in recent years,' wrote Dr. J. H. Jowett, 'by one refrain which I have found running through many biographies. Dr. Parker repeated again and again, "Preach to broken hearts!" And here is the testimony of Ian Maclaren: "The chief end of preaching is comfort. . . ." Never can I forget what a distinguished scholar, who used to sit in my church, once said to me: "Your best work in the pulpit has been to put heart into men for the coming week!" And may I bring you an almost bleeding passage from Dr. Dale: "People want to be comforted. . . . They need consolation — really need it, and do not merely long for it".'[7]

A Father's Simplicity

Thirdly, a father's love will make us simple in our teaching. With what patient simplicity does a father spell out the alphabet to his child! He humbles himself to the child's level. He forgets about his own intellectual accomplishments, his erudition, his prizes and his doctorates, and he is quite content to go back to the rudiments of learning for his child's sake. We must do the same, if we would be true 'fathers' to our people. If we love them, our objective will not be to impress them with our learning but to help them with theirs. While they are still children, we must feed them with milk. J. C. Ryle, formerly Bishop of Liverpool, has asserted that one of the secrets of the evangelical revival

7. *The Preacher, His Life and Work* (Garden City, N. Y.: Doubleday, 1929), p. 107.

in eighteenth century England was that its leaders preached simply. 'To attain this' he wrote, 'they were not ashamed to crucify their style, and to sacrifice their reputation for learning. . . . They carried out the maxim of Augustine: "A wooden key is not so beautiful as a golden one, but if it can open the door when the golden one cannot, it is far more useful".'[8] In order to enforce this truth, Bishop Ryle quotes several other Christian leaders. Luther said, 'No one can be a good preacher to the people who is not willing to preach in a manner that seems childish and vulgar to some'.[9] Again, 'To make easy things hard,' said James Ussher, seventeenth century Archbishop of Armagh, 'is every man's work; but to make hard things easy is the work of a great preacher'.[10] John Wesley wrote in his preface to a volume of sermons, 'I design plain truth for plain people . . . I labour to avoid all words which are not easy to be understood. . .'.[11] And William Grimshaw deliberately preached his sermons in the village church of Haworth in what he used to term 'market language'.[12]

Or, to come to our own day, I have several times heard Dr. Billy Graham say, and justly, that the trouble with us ministers is that we tend to preach to one another! We little realize how unintelligible we often are. 'How much of what is customary to the man in the pulpit', wrote Dr. R. W. Luxton, a consultant physician, in an article in the British Medical Journal in 1957, 'is gibberish to the man in the pew? I was told of a patient in the chapel of a mental hospital who, after listening for a time to the Chaplain, was heard to remark, "There, but for the grace of God, go I"!' The simplicity and directness of Dr. Graham's own preaching are a model for us all, and were recognized by Dr. Geoffrey

8. J. C. Ryle, *The Christian Leaders of England in the* 18th *Century* (1868), London: Chas. S. Thynne Popular Edition (1902), pp. 24, 25.
9. *Ibid.*, p. 25.
10. *Ibid.*, p. 52.
11. *Ibid.*, p. 89.
12. *Ibid.*, p. 116.

Fisher, former Archbishop of Canterbury, who wrote in the June 1954 edition of *Canterbury Diocesan Notes* this comment on the Greater London Crusade: 'The churches . . . expect people to understand whole sentences of church life and doctrine before they have been taught the letters of the Christian alphabet and the words of one syllable. It is the natural mistake of the keen teacher. Dr. Graham has taught us all to begin again at the beginning in our evangelism and speak by the power of the Holy Spirit of sin and of righteousness and of judgment'.[13]

Simplicity in preaching will begin with our subject matter. We shall need to spend most of our time expounding the central themes of the gospel; the more abstruse matters of prophecy, and questions of a controversial or speculative character we can well afford to leave on one side. Then our style should be as simple as our subject. An involved syntax with subordinate clauses in rich abundance may be suitable for the pen; it is certainly out of place in the pulpit. Full stops are better than commas in the spoken word. A staccato style is best. 'Preach,' said Bishop Ryle, 'as if you were asthmatical'. To a simple subject and a simple style add simple words. There is no point in speaking as if we have swallowed a dictionary. Our vocabulary can be rich (for we must avoid stale clichés) without being abstruse. And we must keep clear of jargon. Of course the congregation must come to learn the meaning of great words like 'justification' and 'propitiation', but at first we shall have even to explain what the Bible means by monosyllables like 'grace' and 'faith,' 'hope' and 'love'. If we are wise, we shall take nothing for granted. At least in these days, were we to know the truth, I believe the ignorance of most lay people would astonish us. 'There has never been a time,' wrote *The Times* just after the publication in 1957 of Professor F. L. Cross's *Oxford Dictionary of the Christian Church*, 'in which so many educated people have known so little about Christianity.'

13. Quoted by Frank Colquhoun in *Harringay Story* (London: Hodder & Stoughton, 1954), p. 190.

There is much more that could be said about simplicity in preaching, — about the breaking up of the sermon into sections or divisions, and about the use of repetition and illustration, but I will content myself with one other point, and that is the use of pictorial language. We are accustomed to the use of visual aids in the teaching of the young. In this respect people of all ages are children. We learn and remember so much more readily through our eyes than our ears. But it is not necessary to have actual visual aids for adults if we can enable them to visualize what we are talking about. Children have a vivid, concrete imagination. When they grow up, they fortunately do not lose it altogether. Then let us not be afraid of appealing to people's powers of imagination. As the eastern proverb goes, 'he is the eloquent man, who turns his hearers' ears into eyes, and makes them see what he speaks of'.[14] Jesus did this constantly not only by His parables but by His language, and we must learn to do the same.

A Father's Earnestness

Fourthly, a father's love will make us earnest in our appeal. 'O mamma', cried a little girl, on hearing Charles Simeon preach for the first time in Cambridge, 'what is the gentleman in a passion about?'[15] I have already said something, in chapter 2, about the earnestness of the herald's appeal. Earnestness is a characteristic of the father also. Can he see his children begin to go astray and remain coolly indifferent? Does he see them in danger and give them no warning? A father who loves, cares; and a father who cares will not hesitate to use entreaty if he has cause for anxiety about his children. Paul was a true father to his children. During his three years in Ephesus, he says, he

14. Bishop J. C. Ryle, *Light from Old Times* (London: Thynne & Jarvis, 1890, fifth Ed.), p. 407.
15. Constance E. Padwick, *Henry Martyn* (1922), London: I.V.F. new ed., p. 37.

'did not cease night or day to admonish every one with tears' (Acts 20:31). When did we last weep in spiritual anguish over some soul? 'Dr. Dale of Birmingham was at first inclined to look with disfavour on Mr. Moody. He went to hear him, and his opinion was altered. He regarded him ever after with profound respect and considered that he had a right to preach the gospel "because he could never speak of a lost soul without tears in his eyes".'[16]

Just as the father warns his children of danger, the faithful preacher will sometimes preach of sin, judgment and hell. His ministry will be balanced. He will seek to make known both 'the kindness and the severity of God' (Rom. 11:22), the certainty of judgment as well as the greatness of salvation. It is no mark of love to leave men alone in their peril. If they are perishing without Christ, then we must solemnly warn them of future judgment and earnestly entreat them to flee to 'Jesus who delivers us from the wrath to come' (1 Thess. 1:10). I have always liked the definition of preaching given by Professor Chad Walsh, when he writes: 'The true function of a preacher is to disturb the comfortable and to comfort the disturbed'.[17] We have already thought about men's need of comfort, as there is so much to disturb us in these days. But there are others who are not disturbed when they should be. They are self-satisfied and self-sufficient. They feel no need for God and have no thought of judgment and eternal destiny. Can we abandon them in their fool's paradise? Surely it is our duty to seek by all legitimate means to wake them from their perilous sleep. Of course if we are men-pleasers and care most of all for our reputation, we shall ignore such distasteful subjects. We shall be like the false prophets who said 'Peace, peace' when there was no peace, and God will require the blood of lost souls at our hand (see Ezek. 33:1-9).

16. Quoted by David Smith in the *Expositor's Greek Testament* (London: Hodder & Stoughton, 1910) with reference to 2 John 12.
17. Chad Walsh, *Campus Gods on Trial* (New York: Macmillan, 1953), p. 95.

But if we love other people more than we love our own name, we shall proclaim the wrath of God upon sin as well as the grace of God to sinners. And preaching it out of love, we shall preach it in love, for we dare not preach such things with callous harshness or unfeeling non-chalance. And if we preach in love, the people will pay attention. Children will not turn a deaf ear to their parents' stern warning if they are sure their parents love them. So our people will listen to our words if they see tears in our eyes. They will say to themselves of their minister, not only 'he understands us', but 'he loves us'. As Bishop Ryle wrote of George Whitfield, 'They could not hate the man who wept so much over their souls,' and added: 'Once become satisfied that a man loves you, and you will listen gladly to anything he has to say'.[18] So let love put earnestness into our appeal! If I may quote again from Richard Baxter's great book *The Reformed Pastor*: 'Whatever you do, let the people see that you are in good earnest. . . . How few ministers do preach with all their might. . . . Alas! we speak so drowsily or gently, that sleeping sinners cannot hear. The blow falls so light that hard-hearted persons cannot feel it. . . . What excellent doctrines some ministers have in hand, and let it die in their hands for want of close and lively application. . . . O Sirs, how plainly, how closely and earnestly should we deliver a message of such nature as ours is, when the everlasting life or death of men is concerned in it. . . . What! speak coldly for God and for men's salvation? . . . . Such a work as preaching for men's salvation should be done with all our might — that the people can feel us preach when they hear us'.[19]

A Father's Example

Fifthly, a father's love will make us consistent in our example. This is another aspect of our subject which is not

18. Bishop J. C. Ryle, *The Christian Leaders of England in the 18th Century* (1868), Popular Edition (1902), p. 55.
19. Richard Baxter, *The Reformed Pastor*, (1656), London: Epworth Press (1950), 2nd ed. rev., pp. 145, 106.

strictly relevant to homiletics; and yet we cannot isolate the pulpit or divorce what the preacher says from what he is. The wise parent watches his behaviour and takes great pains to set his children a good and consistent example in all things. He knows the almost frightening power of example for good or ill, of which the Scripture has much to say. He remembers the severe words of Jesus about 'offences', about causing 'one of these little ones . . . to sin', and how 'it would be better for him to have a great millstone fastened round his neck and to be drowned in the depth of the sea' (Mt. 18:6, 7). But if a bad example is corrupting, a good example can uplift and inspire. Paul knew this. As soon as he had declared himself the father of these Corinthians, he went on: 'I urge you, then, be imitators of me' (1 Cor. 4:16). It takes a high degree of self-confidence of the right kind to invite people to follow your example, but Paul did it several times in his epistles. The preacher will no doubt be too modest to do so, but whether he does so or not, the congregation *will* follow him to some extent. He is the only official representative of the Christian faith whom many of them know. They are bound to take a lead from him, not only as they listen to his sermons but as they look at his life. He cannot give himself the luxury of unguarded moments; like his Master he is being watched all the time. It is much easier to lay down the law from the pulpit than to exemplify it in the home. We find it simpler to give directions about the way than to lead others in the way ourselves. But Peter's instruction to us is clear: 'Tend the flock of God that is your charge, . . . not as domineering over those in your charge but being examples to the flock' (1 Pet. 5:2, 3). This is the alternative before us — either 'lords', dogmatic, overbearing, bossy, or 'examples,' humbly seeking to show the way. I think it was Dean Inge who first used the illuminating epigram that 'Christianity is caught not taught'. It is a contagion which spreads by contact with a shining example; it is not just learned from a textbook. God's most powerful visual aid in the education of mankind is a consistent Christian.

So our life must conform to our profession, lest we do not practice what we preach. Richard Baxter can give us good advice in this also, when he describes the great hindrance to the work if we contradict ourselves, 'If your actions give your tongue the lie, and if you build up an hour or two with your mouths, and all the week after pull down with your hands! . . . . He that means as he speaks will surely do as he speaks. . . . It is a palpable error in those ministers that make such disproportion between their preaching and their living, that they will study hard to preach exactly and study little or not at all to live exactly. All the week long is little enough how to speak two hours; and yet one hour seems too much to study how to live all the week. . . . A practical doctrine must be practically preached. We must study as hard how to live well as how to preach well. . . .'[20]

A Father's Prayers

Sixthly, a father's love will make us conscientious in our prayers. I cannot imagine a Christian father who does not pray conscientiously for his family; yet how few preachers pray systematically for their people, like fathers for their children! Praying and preaching go hand in hand. I do not just mean by this that our sermons must be begotten and nurtured by prayer, or that we must pray for ourselves before we mount the pulpit steps, but that we must pray for those to whom we preach. It cannot have escaped us how the Lord Jesus would spend the day preaching and teaching, and then go out into the hills alone to pray for those to whom He had ministered; nor with what regularity St. Paul assured his friends whom he instructed in his epistles that he also prayed for them, yes all of them, and that without ceasing. This is the balanced ministry, to 'devote ourselves to prayer and to the ministry of the word' (Acts 6:4).

And only love will make us thus diligent, for prayer is hard work and secret work. Because it is an exacting ministry,

20. *Ibid.,* p. 162.

we shall only make time for it if we love people enough not to deny them its benefit. Because it is secret and therefore unrewarded by men, we shall only undertake it if we long for their spiritual welfare more than for their thanks. Paul could write: 'Brethren, my heart's desire and prayer to God for Israel is, that they might be saved' (Rom. 10:1, A.V.). This is the meaning of prayer. It is an expression of the heart's desire. Intercession is impossible without love. Let Richard Baxter put it succinctly for us: 'Prayer must carry on our work as well as preaching: he preacheth not heartily to his people, that will not pray for them. . .'.[21]

We do not have this love for people by nature; we can only receive it by grace. By nature we are selfish, lazy and hungry for the praise of men. There is only one way to learn to love, and that is, to yearn for people, in St. Paul's phrase, 'with the affection of Christ Jesus' (Phil. 1:8). If His unsearchable, unquenchable love for people could fill us, we could love them with His love. And such love, utterly unself-regarding, preoccupied only with the positive good of others even at a cost to ourselves, will make us care for our people, as a father cares for his children. Such love will make us understanding and gentle, simple and earnest, consistent in our example and conscientious in our prayers.

21. *Ibid.,* p. 137.

CHAPTER FIVE

A SERVANT

The Preacher's Power and Motive

IN referring to the preacher as a 'servant', I have in mind one particular verse of Scripture (and the whole context in which it is found), namely, 1 Corinthians 3:5, where St. Paul writes: 'What then is Apollos?   What is Paul?   *Servants* through whom you believed, as the Lord assigned to each'.

In many ways the Corinthian church gave remarkable evidence of the active grace of God.   Some of its members, now 'washed . . . sanctified . . . justified' (1 Cor. 6:11), had been redeemed from the depths of sin, and others had been marvellously 'enriched' by Christ 'with all speech and all knowledge', so that they were 'not lacking in any spiritual gift' (1 Cor. 1:5, 7).   Yet the church's inner life seems to have been grievously contaminated by sin and error, and, in particular, the congregation was torn by bitter factions. 'There is quarrelling among you, my brethren,' Paul had to write.   'What I mean is that each one of you says, "I belong to Paul", or "I belong to Apollos", or "I belong to Cephas", or "I belong to Christ" ' (1 Cor. 1:11, 12).   There is no evidence in the epistle that these divisions were doctrinal and that each party held a different theological position.   Rather does the Apostle trace the Corinthian rivalries to what we would call a personality cult.   The Christians were showing an exaggerated deference to certain well-known church leaders and drawing odious comparisons between them.   St. Paul is horrified by what he hears.   He sees that these Corinthian Christians are giving to mere men an allegiance which is due to Christ alone.   'Was Paul crucified for you?' he asks in amazement, meaning, 'Are you putting your trust in *me,*

as if it were I who died to be your Saviour?' Again, 'Were
you baptized into the name of Paul?' (1 Cor. 1:13, literally).
That is, 'Did your baptism signify your initiation into fellowship with me?'. Christian conversion and Christian baptism
both have Christ Himself as their focus. Conversion is faith
in Christ; baptism is the sacrament of incorporation into
Christ. How dare these Corinthians speak and act as if
sinful, mortal men were the objects of their faith and baptism?
And how can they employ party solgans which imply that
they 'belong' to human leaders like Paul, Peter and Apollos?
The truth is, as he goes on to write, that if anybody may be
said to 'belong' to anybody, then the minister belongs to the
congregation, not the congregation to the minister: 'Let none
boast of men. For all things are yours, whether Paul or
Apollos or Cephas . . . all are yours (cf. 1 Cor. 1:12, 3:4 with
3:21, 22).

The shameful cult of human personalities which tarnished
the life of the first century Corinthian church still persists in
Christendom, and a most improper and unbecoming regard is
paid to some church leaders today. I do not mean to imply
that the Christian ministry is not an honourable vocation.
Of course it is. Indeed, the Scripture commands us to 'obey',
'submit to' and 'respect' our spiritual pastors, and 'to esteem
them very highly in love because of their work' (Heb. 13:17;
1 Thess. 5:12, 13). But this quotation makes it plain that we
are humbly to honour them for the divine office which they
hold; it does not mean that we are to fawn upon them personally, or that we are to allow others to fawn upon us. We
must never show a reverence to ecclesiastical dignitaries which
is due to God alone. Preachers are specially exposed to the
danger of flattery. I fear that the whole frame of mind in
which some Christian people go to church is wrong. They do
not go to worship *God* or to hear *God's* Word. They go to
hear a man. So it is not the message to which they listen, but
the oratory. They savour the sermon with their minds
as if they relished some tasty morsel in their mouths. They
say afterwards how much they enjoyed or did not enjoy it.

But sermons are not intended to be 'enjoyed'. Their purpose is to give *profit* to the hearers, not *pleasure*. Sermons are not artistic creations to be critically evaluated for their form. They are 'tools, and not works of art'. A sermon is never an end in itself, but a means to an end, the end being 'saving souls'.[1] I have no hesitation in saying that people who 'congratulate' a preacher on his sermon, and preachers who expect such congratulation from their people, are alike most offensive to God. Men are called to preach not themselves but Christ Jesus as Saviour and Lord (1 Cor. 1:23; 2 Cor. 4:5). What matters, therefore, is Christ Himself who is proclaimed, and not the men who proclaim Him. To think or act otherwise is not only to usurp God's glory, but to jeopardize the preacher's whole ministry, bringing it first into discredit and finally to ruin.

The Apostle Paul saw with crystalline clarity the offence and the danger of the Corinthians' behaviour. As a result, he wrote with great vehemence against it. It was clear evidence of their babyish immaturity and of their carnality, he said. Their outlook was not God's but man's (1 Cor. 3:1-4). And he proceeded to call them to a better mind. The excessive and misguided loyalty which they were giving to certain leaders was due to their false view of the ministry. If only they would cultivate a sober, seemly and balanced view of the Christian ministry, they would be protected from idly boasting of men. Thus, he cries out 'What then is Apollos? What is Paul?' It is to be noted that he does not even ask 'Who is Apollos? Who is Paul?' He is determined to speak of himself and Apollos disdainfully, almost disrespectfully. So he uses the neuter; as much as to say: 'What on earth do you think we are, that you should attach such importance to us?' The question is no sooner asked than answered. We are mere servants, he asserts, servants of Jesus the Lord, and what glory is due to servants? We are 'ser-

1. Phillips Brooks, *Lectures on Preaching* (London: H. R. Allenson, 1895), p. 112.

vants through whom you believed, as the Lord assigned to each' (1 Cor. 3:5), having stated this, Paul enlarges on the correct view of the Christian ministry throughout this and the following chapters of his epistle.

Several Greek words are translated 'servant' in the English Bible. There is *oiketēs*, the domestic or household servant of whom we spoke in Chapter 1. There is *doulos*, the bond slave, who has no legal rights and belongs to his master as a personal possession. There is also *hupēretēs*, which occurs in the next chapter (4:11), which meant originally one who rowed in the lower tier of a war galley, an underoarsman, hence an 'underling' or 'subordinate'. But the word Paul uses here is *diakonos*, which in the New Testament has both a special and a general sense. In its special sense, it means a 'deacon', being so translated in three passages (Phil. 1:1; 1 Tim. 3:8, 10, 12, 13; Rom. 16:1), or, less particularly, what we would call an ordained minister (2 Cor. 3:6, 4:4, 11: 23; Eph. 3:7; Col. 1:23, 25; 1 Tim. 4:6). But it does not seem to bear this meaning here, and, as Bishop Westcott wrote, 'there is no evidence that at this time *diakonia* and *diakonein* had an exclusively official sense'. These words are, in fact, employed frequently in the New Testament to describe in general 'the work of ministry' (Eph. 4:12), to which all Christians are called. We are both servants of Christ (e.g., John 12:26) and servants of men (e.g., Mk. 9:35, 10:43). According to the Grimm-Thayer lexicon, the *diakonos* is 'one who executes the commands of another, especially of a master; a servant, attendant, minister'. There seem to be two elements in the word, first of personal service and, secondly, of service undertaken at another's command. The element of personal service is clear in Martha who 'served' in the socalled 'ministering women', in Peter's mother-in-law after her fever had been cured (Lk. 10:40; John 12:2; Lk. 8:3; Mk. 15:41; Lk. 4:39), and in such practical help as was given by Onesimus and Onesiphorus to Paul, and by Paul in his collection for the poverty stricken Judaean Christians (Philem. 13; 2 Tim. 1:16-18; Rom. 15:25; cf. 10:23, 25). That *diakonia* was normally undertaken at the command, and on the authority, of somebody else is suggested by the use of *diakonos* to describe a king's attendants, the waiters who served food and drink at the wedding feast in Cana, and even the magistrate who acts as 'God's servant' (Mt. 22:13; John 2:5, 9; Rom. 13:4). In none of these instances is the *diakonos* working in his private capacity; he is the representative of a higher authority whose commission and command he is fulfilling. He is acting in his master's name, and thus his master is acting through him.

It appears to be with this emphasis that the Apostle uses word here. We are, he writes, 'servants through whom you believed', that is, through whom our Master was at work to arouse faith in you. The preposition *through*, in the context of these early chapters of 1 Corinthians, has an important significance. We are not servants, '*from* whom you believed', as if preachers were the authors of men's faith, quickening and evoking it. Nor are we servants *in* whom you believed, as if preachers were the objects of men's faith. As we have already seen, it is in or into Christ that men believe and are baptized. The ministry of both Word and Sacrament sets forth Jesus Christ as the sole object of faith (cf. 1 Cor. 1:13-15, 2:5). Instead, we are 'servants *through* whom you believed', the agents through whom God works, or the instruments by which He arouses faith in the hearers of the Word. The function of the preacher, as of John the Baptist, is 'to bear witness to the light, that all might believe *through* him' (John 1:7).

This truth of the preacher as an agent, a servant through whom God works, is one we began to consider in Chapter 2, in which we thought of the preacher as an ambassador through whom God addresses His appeal to men (2 Cor. 5:20). That men can be channels of God's grace and power is suggested many times in the New Testament (e.g., Acts 15:12, 'through them'; cf. Acts 14:27, 'with them'). But what is meant by this idea is more elaborately worked out by St. Paul in 1 Corinthians 3. We are 'servants through whom you believed, as the Lord assigned to each'. That is, each servant has a different task assigned to him, but the Lord works through each. The particular assignments of Paul and Apollos are now described. 'I planted, Apollos watered, but God gave the growth' (1 Cor. 3:6). The Apostle resorts to a simple agricultural metaphor. The Corinthian church is 'God's field' (1 Cor. 3:9), but, although the field was His, he permitted men to labour in it.

It was Paul himself, visiting Corinth on his first missionary journey, who did the initial planting. Apollos followed him to water what he had sown. Nevertheless, though Paul 'planted' and Apollos 'watered' (both verbs are aorists, describing the finishing of a stage), it was God who 'gave the growth'. In contrast to the other verbs, this is an imperfect, indicating God's continuing activity. Men came and went, but all the time God Himself was causing the seed to spring up, to grow and to blossom. This being the case, 'neither he who plants nor he who waters is anything, but only God who gives the growth' (1 Cor. 3:7).

> *We plough the fields, and scatter*
> *The good seed on the land;*
> *But it is fed and watered*
> *By God's almighty hand.*

And what is true of material seed applies with equal force to the seed of God's Word. We are privileged to sow and water, but all our labour will be vain unless God gives the increase. The preacher is a divine agent or *diakonos*, and all his service will be lost if God the Lord does not work powerfully through him to create faith in the hearers of the word. Our subject, then, in this final chapter, is the preacher and the power of God.

The Need of Power

We must begin by reminding ourselves of the urgent and indispensable need for God's power in preaching. I hope we are all oppressed by the spectacle of the Church's power-

lessness today. We thank God that in some parts of the
world God is manifesting His power to save. But in too
many areas, especially in the older, historic Churches, there
are few signs of life or power. There may be large atten-
dances, great social activity, and a busy programme, but
there is little power. In my own country at least, if one
is honest, the Church makes little impact on the nation as a
whole. The masses of the people are ignorant of the gospel
or indifferent to it. They regard the Church as out-of-date
and irrelevant, a curious anachronistic survival from an earlier
age. To them the Church is impotent, decadent. And if
the Church at large lacks power, what about our own ministry? Are men and women being converted through our
preaching? Not emotionally stirred and superficially affected,
but deeply and permanently regenerated by the gracious work
of the Holy Spirit? If only the pulpits of the world were
occupied by men 'clothed with power from on high' (Lk.
24:49), we should prove again that 'the gospel . . .is the power
of God for salvation to every one who has faith, to the Jew
first and also to the Greek' (Rom. 1:16).

The first step towards such an enduement with power is
the humble acknowledgment of our lack of it. If one may
generalize, the churches are busy using statistics to pull the
wool over their own eyes. We seem unwilling to admit the
grievously weak state of the Church today. We are content
to judge with man's judgment, and to look on outward
appearances only. Consequently, we do not see the worldli-
ness of the Church, the lack of a conviction of sin and of a
vision of God, the externalism of much of our worship, the
shallowness of our fellowship, our disobedience in the matter
of evangelism, and the poor approximation of our lives to the
standard of meekness and holiness set before us in the
Beatitudes.

We need power not only in our lives, but in our ministry.
As preachers we shall never begin to seek the power of God
until we have come to see the futility of attempting to proclaim God's Word in man's weakness alone. The folly of it

appears when we consider the biblical estimate of the depraved condition of man, who is altogether beyond the reach of merely human enlightenment or persuasion, and will only respond to the lifegiving power of God. Thus, the Scripture teaches clearly that man in his natural state, unredeemed and unregenerate, is blind. 'The god of this world has blinded the minds of the unbelievers, to keep them from seeing the light of the gospel of the glory of Christ, who is the likeness of God' (2 Cor. 4:4). How then can any man see and believe? In order to answer this question, St. Paul draws an analogy between the old creation and the new. He sends our thoughts racing back millions of years to the primeval chaos, when 'the earth was without form and void, and darkness was upon the face of the deep' (Gen. 1:2). All was shapeless, lifeless, cheerless, dark and void, until God's creative word brought light and warmth, shape and beauty. So it is with the Christless heart of the natural man. The dim twilight of nature (his reason and conscience) just relieves the otherwise impenetrable gloom, but all is dark, void and chill until God's dramatic fiat causes a new creation. 'For it is the God who said "let light shine out of darkness", who has shone in our hearts to give the light of the knowledge of the glory of God in the face of Christ' (2 Cor. 4:6).

Men are not only blind, but dead — 'dead in trespasses and sins', 'alienated from the life of God because of the ignorance that is in them, due to their hardness of heart' (Eph. 2:1, A.V.; 4:18). Jesus Himself taught the same thing. 'Truly, truly I say to you, he who hears my word and believes Him who sent me, has eternal life; he does not come into judgment, but has passed from death to life' (John 5:24). If those who hear and believe thereby pass from death to life, it is plain that they are previously dead.

This, then, is the state of unredeemed man according to the Scriptures. He is both sightless and lifeless, both blind and dead. How can we reach him? Are we so foolish as to imagine that we can somehow, by our own argument or rhetoric, induce within him either spiritual understanding or life? No. It is not given to us to give sight to the blind or life to the dead. God alone is the author of light and life. Jesus Christ is the same yesterday, today and forever, and He who opened blind eyes and raised the dead, is able to do so today. Only His touch can cause the scales to fall from men's eyes. Only His voice can summon the dead from the tomb (John 5:25).

Granted that only the power of God can make the blind see and the dead live, where is this power to be found? How can preachers become such channels of it as to be 'servants through whom' others will believe? There is no clearer exposition in the New Testament of the place of divine power than 1 Corinthians 1:17 — 2:5. It is, perhaps, the passage of Scripture which preachers should read and study more than any other, and by which we should judge and reform our ministry.

There are five references in this passage to *dunamis*, power, and particularly to *dunamis Theou*, the power of God. The Apostle fears lest 'the cross of Christ be emptied of its *power*' (v. 17), and twice he states that 'the word of the cross' or of 'Christ crucified' is 'to those who are called', and are therefore 'being saved', 'the *power* of God' (1:18, 23, 24). Further, he is anxious to proclaim this message 'not in plausible words of wisdom, but in demonstration of the Spirit and *power*', so that men's 'faith might not rest in the wisdom of men but in the *power* of God' (2:4, 5).

Where this divine power resides is already implicit in the verse with which the passage opens:[2] *Christ did not send me to baptize but to preach the gospel, and not with eloquent wisdom, lest the cross of Christ be emptied of its power* (v. 17). In these words Paul introduces us both to the origin of our message (good news is entrusted to us to make known), to the substance of it (it is good news of the cross of Christ) and to the manner of its proclamation (*not with eloquent*

2. Words quoted in this chapter from 1 Cor. 1:17 — 2:5 are all printed in italics, so that the exposition may be more readily followed.

wisdom). We must carefully consider what further the Apostle has to say about these three aspects of the preaching ministry. Perhaps I may attempt to summarize it in three propositions.

The Word of God

First, there is power in the Word of God. Power for salvation is not in man's wisdom but in God's Word. If men would be saved, therefore, it is to God's Word that they must turn; and if preachers would exercise a saving ministry it is God's Word which they must preach. The Apostle draws a clear distinction between divine and human wisdom. He quotes from Jehovah's message of judgment upon 'the wise men' of Judah in Isaiah's day (Is. 29:14) and says: *It is written, I will destroy the wisdom of the wise, and the cleverness of the clever I will thwart* (v. 19). And he goes on: *Where is the wise man? Where is the scribe? Where is the debater of this age? Has not God made foolish the wisdom of the world?* (v. 20). What was true of Judah in the eighth century B.C. was true of Corinth in the first century A.D. God's attitude to intellectual arrogance has not changed. Man cannot find God by his own wisdom. God is infinite and therefore unknowable by the effort of man's mind. God must Himself take the initiative to speak and to save, and this He has graciously done: *For since, in the wisdom* of God, the world did not know God through wisdom, it *pleased God through the folly of what we preach to save those who believe* (v. 21). God's pleasure and purpose are here plainly stated in the negative and positive counterparts of this striking verse. Negatively, *in the wisdom of God the World did not know God through wisdom.* That is, the wisdom of man has been set aside by the wisdom of God. God has in His wisdom decreed that no man shall find Him or know Him by his own human wisdom. There is no power in the mind of finite, fallen man to discover or fathom God. God is altogether beyond man's reach. Therefore, positively, *it pleased God* to supply man's lack, and to do it *through the folly of what we preach*, that is, through the *kērygma*. Through this message, which is foolish in the eyes of the world, it is God's will *to save those who believe*.

It is important to observe the vivid contrasts which the Apostle draws in this statement. First, there is an intended contrast between the verbs *to know* and *to save*. It is God's pleasure not just that men should know Him, but that He should save them. Intellectual enlightenment is not enough; salvation from sin is our preeminent need. Next, God wills to bring us to this saving knowledge of Himself, not by our own wit or wisdom but through His word, not by human reason but by divine revelation, by the gospel, the *kērygma*. Thirdly, God's plan is to save through the gospel not those who are clever and learned, but *those who believe*. The condition of salvation is faith, not intellectual brilliance.

The Apostle proceeds to enforce these general truths with a more particular reference to Jews and Greeks. *Jews demand signs*, he writes, *and Greeks seek wisdom, but we preach Christ crucified* (vv. 22, 23). Notice the verbs in this sentence. *The Jews* were making imperious demands, insisting on certain signs before they were prepared to accept the claims of Jesus. *The Greeks* were for ever restlessly seeking and searching for wisdom. *But we preach* . . . that is, our task as Christian preachers is not subserviently to answer all the questions which men put to us; nor to attempt to meet all the demands which are made on us; nor hesitantly to make tentative suggestions to the philosophically minded; but rather to proclaim a message which is dogmatic because it is divine. The preacher's responsibility is proclamation, not discussion. There is too much discussion of the Christian religion today, particularly with unbelievers, as if we were more concerned with men's opinions of Christ than with the honour and glory of Jesus Christ Himself. Are we to cast our Priceless Pearl before swine to let them sniff at Him and trample upon Him at their pleasure? No. We are called to proclaim Christ, not to discuss Him. As we have already seen, we are 'heralds', charged to publish abroad a message which did not originate with us (that we should presume to tamper with it) but with Him who gave it us to publish. It is here described as glad tidings (v. 17), the *kērygma* (vv. 21, 24) and the 'testimony' or 'mystery' of God.[3] To this revealed message men must humbly submit. 'If any one among you thinks that he is wise in this age, let him become a fool that he may become wise (1 Cor. 2:18). I believe that this 'let him become a fool' is one of the hardest words of Scripture to the proud hearts and minds of men. Like the brilliant intellectuals of ancient Greece our contemporaries have unbounded confidence in the human reason. They want to think their way to God by themselves, and to gain credit for discovering God by their own effort. But God resists such swellings of pride on the part of the finite creature. Of course men have been given minds to use, as we have seen in previous chapters, and they are never to stifle or smother them, but they must humble them reverently before the revelation of God, becoming in Paul's word 'fools' and in Christ's word 'babes' (Mt. 6:25). It is only babes to whom God reveals Himself and only fools whom He makes wise.

So, if the sinner must humble himself to receive God's Word, the preacher must humble himself to proclaim it. There is power in it. It is 'like fire, . . . like a hammer which breaks the rock in pieces' (Jer. 23:29). Again, 'The word of God is living and active, sharper than any two-edged sword, piercing to the division of soul and spirit, of joints and marrow, and discerning the thoughts and intentions of the heart' (Heb. 4:12). But let it not be thought that its power is principally destructive, like a burning fire, a smashing hammer, or a piercing sword. The gospel is, above all, 'the power of God for salvation' (Rom. 1:16). There is no stronger argument for faithful expository preaching than this, that it is through the *kērygma*, the revealed good news committed to our trust, that God is pleased *to save those who*

3. Alternative readings of 2:1.

believe. There is no saving power in the words of men. The devil does not relinquish his grasp upon his prisoners at the bidding of mere mortals. No word has authority for him but the Word of God. Then let us proclaim and expound God's Word, confident that it 'effectually worketh' (1 Thess. 2:13, A.V.) in those who believe.

The Cross of Christ

The second proposition which we may derive from this passage is that there is power in the cross of Christ. The Word of God is *the word of the cross* (v. 18). The *kērygma* through which God saves *those who believe* is *Christ crucified* (vv. 21, 23). It was on the cross that Jesus Christ bore our sins and broke the power of the enemy (e.g., 1 Pet. 2:24; Col. 2:15; Heb. 2:14), and it is therefore only by the cross that men and women are personally delivered from sin and Satan. It is Christ crucified in whom they must put their trust; it is, therefore, Christ crucified whom we must proclaim.

In this century, as in the first, however, we shall find that there are many who see in the cross no divine wisdom or power. It causes them to stumble rather than to rise, to be confused rather than to be enlightened. *We preach Christ crucified, a stumbling block to Jews and folly to Gentiles, but to those who are called, both Jews and Greeks, Christ the power of God and the wisdom of God* (vv. 23, 24). What was *a stumbling block to Jews* (v. 23) is still offensive to their spiritual progeny, those imbued with a legalistic spirit who, 'ignorant of the righteousness that comes from God', are 'seeking to establish their own' and will not submit to His (Rom. 10:3). To all those who take pride in their own morality and imagine that they can win salvation by their own merit, the cross will ever remain *skandalon*, a stumbling block. It grievously wounds their pride. From the cross Christ seems to say to them: 'I am here because of your sins. If you could save yourself, I should not need to be here.' Faced with this dilemma, the moralist must either renounce his own righteousness and thankfully embrace Christ's, or proudly cling to his own and repudiate God's gracious offer in Christ.

The cross is also *folly to Gentiles* (v. 23) or *Greeks* (vv. 22, 24). If the Jews passion was righteousness, the Greek's was reason. So while the Jew represents the moralist or legalist who takes pride in his own character, the Greek stands for the intellectualist whose boast is in his wisdom. The cross was *skandalon* to the former, and *mōria*, foolishness, to the latter. It is well known how ludicrous it appeared to the Gentile mind that men should worship a God who died in shame on a Roman gallows. According to Origen, the second century pagan philosopher Celsus scornfully referred to Christians as 'actually worshipping a dead man',[4] while a drawing found on the Palatine in Rome gives a cruel caricature of Christian worship as it depicts a slave kneeling before a donkey on a gibbet, with the caption: 'Alexamenos worships God'. The modern mind is no more friendly to the gospel of Christ crucified than was the ancient mind of Greece and Rome. I have myself heard intellectuals contemptuously dismiss the cross as 'a hangover from primitive blood rituals', 'a revolting superstition long ago discarded by enlightened men'.

Are we, then, to change or modify our message simply because it is offensive to man's pride of character and intellect? I have read that the seventeenth century Jesuit missionaries in China did. They were anxious not to offend the refined taste of the Chinese literati. So they redrafted the gospel story omitting everything to which exception might be taken, and especially the crucifixion. It is not surprising that what was left, described by Professor Hugh Trevor-Roper, Regius Professor of Modern History at Oxford, as an 'unobjectionable residue', had no divine power in it to win lasting converts.

Nor need we expect any results if we ourselves deny, or

4. *Contra Celsum.*

fail to preach to others, the faith of Christ crucified. There is power in the cross of Christ. What is *a stumbling block* to some and *folly* to others is yet *to those who are called* (v. 24), and who, having responded to God's call in repentance and faith, *are being saved* (v. 18), *Jews and Greeks,* both *the power of God and the wisdom of God. For the foolishness of God is wiser than men, and the weakness of God is stronger than men* (vv. 24, 25). This is the paradox. What offends the proud, saves the humble. There is wonderful power in the cross of Christ. It has power to wake the dullest conscience and melt the hardest heart; to cleanse the unclean; to reconcile him who is afar off and restore him to fellowship with God; to redeem the prisoner from his bondage and lift the pauper from the dunghill; to break down the barriers which divide men from one another; to transform our wayward characters into the image of Christ and finally make us fit to stand in white robes before the throne of God. All this is the 'salvation' which God works in men and women through the *kērygma* of Christ crucified. *The word of the cross . . . is the power of God* (v. 18). Let us never forget it.

So men and women, who cannot be saved by their own power (as the Jews thought) or by their own wisdom (as the Greeks thought), may be saved by Christ crucified who is the wisdom and power of God. Power and wisdom are in God, not men. Even God's foolishness is wiser, and His weakness stronger, than men. In order to emphasize this truth, that the wisdom and power by which men are saved, come not from themselves but from God in and through Christ, the Apostle now reminds his Corinthian readers of the circumstances of their own conversion. *For consider your call, brethren,* he says; *not many of you were wise according to worldly standards, not many were powerful . . .* (v. 26). Exactly! If men are obsessed with their own power or wisdom, they are not willing humbly to submit themselves to God's. God's power is made perfect in human weakness (cf. 2 Cor. 12:9) and His wisdom in human folly. Therefore He has seldom chosen the naturally wise and powerful among men. Instead, *God chose what is foolish in the world to shame the wise, God chose what is weak in the world to shame the strong, God chose what is low and despised in the world, even things that are not, to bring to nothing things that are* (vv. 27, 28). Why? Paul goes on at once to give the reason: *so that no human being might boast in the presence of God* (v. 29). No man can save himself; only the cross of Christ can save him. Man owes everything to God. As a creature he is entirely dependent upon his Creator, and as a sinner upon his Saviour. To boast of himself, of his wisdom or of his power, is sinful folly. *God*, and God alone, *is the source of your life in Christ Jesus, whom God made our wisdom, our righteousness, and sanctification and redemption* (v. 30). We have no wisdom of our own by which to know God; we need His self-revelation in Christ. And we have no power of ourselves to save ourselves; power for salvation, whether initial justification, progressive sanctification or final redemption, is in Christ alone. Without Him we have neither wisdom nor power. Without Him we are lost. *Therefore*, Paul concludes, *as it is written: let him who boasts, boast of the Lord* (v. 31).

Having argued that saving power is not in the *hearers* of the Word, the Apostle goes on in the early verses of 1 Corinthians 2 to show that it is not in the *preacher* of the Word either. I venture to say that evangelical Christians are stronger in their conviction about the former than the latter. That is to say, we never grow tired of reiterating that no man can be saved by his own works; but do we not sometimes behave and preach as if we thought he could be saved by ours? We must be consistent. If we call on men to renounce their own wisdom and power, in order to embrace Christ, we must beware of parading ours before them as the object of their faith. They must trust neither their own nor ours, but God's only. The Apostle Paul perceived this truth a good deal more clearly than many of us do today. He was determined to humble all men, both others and himself, before God. He was in no doubt that the wisdom to know God and the power to be saved were from God in Christ alone, and neither from man nor in man. So he illustrated his great theme further, not now from the circumstances of his readers' conversion, but from his own experience as a preacher. *When I came to you, brethren,* he continues, *I did not come proclaiming to you the testimony of God in lofty words or wisdom* (v. 1). He did not rely for effect in his preaching either on his own wisdom or on his own power in uttering it. His message and his manner in delivering it were free from the taint of human pride and prowess. What was his message? Not worldly *wisdom,* but rather: *I decided to know nothing among you except Jesus Christ and Him crucified* (v. 2). As for his manner, he eschewed the use of *lofty words* (v. 1). He had repudiated the idea of preaching the gospel *with eloquent wisdom* (1:17). Instead, he goes on: *I was with you in weakness and in much fear and trembling* (v. 3). He had been content, when visiting Corinth, to preach a foolish message in human weakness. The Corinthians had certainly not been brought to a knowledge of God by a display of the Apostle's own wisdom; he had renounced it for the folly of God's *kērygma* concerning Christ crucified. Nor had they been converted by a powerful display of Paul's oratory; but rather by the power of the Holy Spirit.

The Holy Spirit

This brings us to the third proposition which we may draw from this passage, namely that there is power in the Holy Spirit. Let us listen to Paul again, as he proceeds: *My speech and my message were not in plausible words of wisdom, but in demonstration of the Spirit and power* (v. 4). He has already explained what his *message, kērygma,* was, both in origin and in content. It came from God and centered on

Christ. God was its author, and Christ its substance. But still this glorious God-given, Christ-centered gospel could be ineffective. If it were preached *with eloquent wisdom, the cross of Christ* would *be emptied of its power* (v. 17). Paul refused to trust in his own personality or eloquence in seeking to communicate his message to others. He deliberately renounced what he called *plausible words of wisdom* (v. 4). He was no doubt referring to the rhetorical subtleties of the Greek orators, who competed with one another in the skill and polish of their utterances. Instead, he says that his message was delivered *in demonstration of the Spirit and power* (v. 4). That is, he trusted in the powerful demonstration or proof (*apodeixis*) which the Holy Spirit could add to his simple, faltering words. He spoke in such human weakness, that by that alone no man could ever have come to clear understanding or saving faith. But the Holy Spirit took his faithful proclamation of the gospel and carried it home with mighty conviction to the conscience and mind of the hearers so that they saw and believed.

This was no new experience for the Apostle Paul. Already in Thessalonica, on the same second missionary journey, the gospel he preached had gone forth 'not only in word, but also in power and in the Holy Spirit and with full conviction' (1 Thess. 1:5). What was true of Paul's preaching ministry should equally characterize ours. Every preacher who has been endowed with gifts of personality and fluent speech knows the temptation to put his confidence in the power of his own ability. If only he is lucid enough, and eloquent enough, and dogmatic enough and persuasive enough, he can surely induce the people to embrace the salvation of Christ and yield themselves to His allegiance. He may certainly succeed in swaying their emotions and arousing them to action of some kind. But the work will be neither deep nor lasting. Only the Holy Spirit can convict the conscience, illumine the mind, enflame the heart and move the will. Only the powerful demonstration which the Holy Spirit can give to the Word can prevail upon people to receive it, to hold it fast and so to bring forth fruit with patience. This certainly does not mean that we are at liberty to be neglectful of study or careless in preparation. Nor may we conclude that we must always preach extempore and not take pains to choose the words by which to convey our message clearly and forcefully. If the divine inspiration of Scripture extended to the very words used by the human authors (cf. 1 Cor. 2:13), we cannot imagine that the choice of words is unimportant. A precise message can only be communicated in precise language. No; what Paul is emphasizing is that the object of our confidence in the proclamation of the Word is not to be our own strength of personality or argument (however much we may rightly plead and argue with our hearers) but the power of the Holy Spirit.

It is said that Charles Haddon Spurgeon, wonderfully gifted by God as a powerful preacher, used to say to himself over and over again as he slowly mounted the steps to his high pulpit, 'I believe in the Holy Ghost, I believe in the Holy Ghost, I believe in the Holy Ghost'. Spurgeon also wrote: 'The gospel is preached in the ears of all; it only comes with power to some. The power that is in the gospel does not lie in the eloquence of the preacher; otherwise men would be converters of souls. Nor does it lie in the preacher's learning; otherwise it would consist in the wisdom of men. We might preach till our tongues rotted, till we should exhaust our lungs and die, but never a soul would be converted unless there were mysterious power going with it — the Holy Ghost changing the will of man. O Sirs! we might as well preach to stone walls as to preach to humanity unless the Holy Ghost be with the Word, to give it power to convert the soul'.

The three propositions which I have brought to you from the beginning of First Corinthians together indicate that the source of power in preaching is Trinitarian. *Dunamis Theou*, divine power to save, is in the Word of God concerning the

cross of Christ when it is demonstrated or confirmed by the
Holy Spirit. That is to say, the origin, substance and de-
livery of the preacher's message are all alike divine. He is
not at liberty to alter either the matter or the manner of his
preaching. He is commissioned to proclaim God's *kērygma*,
which is Christ crucified, in the power of the Holy Spirit.
It is equally foolish for him to attempt to preach his own
message with divine power as it is to preach God's message
with his own power. His manner must conform to his
matter; he must deliver God's Word in God's way.

It should be clear from this how completely different
Christian preaching is from much secular propaganda. I
do not deny that there may be such a thing as Christian
propaganda and Christian advertising; I am here employing
the word 'propaganda' loosely for the increasingly common
use of the mass media of communication in which the means
are made to serve an unworthy end. The incompatibility
of such methods with true Christian preaching may be
seen in the three spheres which we have been considering,
namely the origin and substance of the message, and the manner employed to communicate it. First, the propagandist
may suppress, distort or embellish the truth; while the
preacher is committed to proclaim faithfully the Word which
has been entrusted to him. Secondly, the propagandist
aims to please, to attract, to curry favour, to win popularity;
while the preacher is committed to preach the message of
Christ crucified which he knows to be offensive to the proud,
a stumbling block to some and folly to others. Thirdly, the
propagandist relies on astute psychological techniques, seeking
to convince and convert by pressure, humour, pathos, deceit,
logic, repetition or flattery; while the preacher is committed
to proclaim a plain message without subtlety, relying on the
invisible power of the Holy Spirit.

Holiness and Humility

There is one last question which must be asked and answered: On what conditions may preachers hope to be vehicles

of this divine power?   We have seen that we must be faithful in handling the Word of God, expounding the Scriptures and preaching the cross, for there is power in God's Word and in Christ's cross.   But how can we become channels for the power of the Holy Spirit?   How can the promise of Jesus be fulfilled that from our innermost being the 'rivers of living water' will flow into the lives of others? (see John 7:38, 39).   I believe there are two essential conditions: holiness and humility.

On the necessity of holiness I will not stay long, for I have referred to it several times in these chapters and Paul does not mention it in the passage we are now studying. Suffice it to say that if any man covets the honour of being 'a vessel for noble use, consecrated and useful to the master of the house, ready for any good work', then he must see to it that he 'purifies himself from what is ignoble' (2 Tim. 2: 21).   None but holy vessels are employed by the Holy One of Israel.   We must heed the memorable words written by Robert Murray McCheyne to the Rev. Dan Edwards on 2 October 1840 after his ordination as a missionary to the Jews: 'I trust you will have a pleasant and profitable time in Germany.   I know you will apply hard to German; but do not forget the culture of the inner man, — I mean of the heart.   How diligently the cavalry officer keeps his sabre clean and sharp; every stain he rubs off with the greatest care. Remember you are God's sword, — His instrument, — I trust a chosen vessel unto Him to bear His name.   In great measure, according to the purity and perfections of the instrument, will be the success.   It is not great talents God blesses so much as great likeness to Jesus.   A holy minister is an awful weapon in the hand of God'.[5]

The second indispensable condition of enjoying the power of the Holy Spirit in preaching is humility, and it is on this that Paul lays his emphasis.   There is unmistakeable teaching

5. Andrew A. Bonar, *Memoir and Remains of R. M. McCheyne* (London: Oliphant, Anderson & Ferrier, new ed., 1892) , p. 282.

here that God's power is revealed through human weakness
and God's wisdom through human folly. It is a principle of
divine activity, which the Apostle sees illustrated both in his
readers' conversion and in his own ministry. God had
chosen weak and foolish things in Corinth, in order to prove
that their salvation was due to His power and wisdom alone.
In just the same way it was through the weakness and folly
of Paul's preaching that God's wisdom and power were made
known. Knowing that he could not win men by his own
wisdom, Paul deliberately renounced it and preached instead
the folly of the *kērygma* (v. 21). Knowing also that men
could not be saved by his own oratorical power, he deliberately renounced this also and went to Corinth *in weakness
and in much fear and trembling* (v. 3). I say again that this
was his deliberate policy. He humbled himself before God
and men. Massive intellect that he had, and keen as he
was to impart wisdom to the mature (1 Cor. 2:6), he yet
intentionally *decided to know nothing* among the then unbelieving Corinthians *except Jesus Christ and Him crucified*
(v. 2). He was willing to be a 'fool for Christ's sake' (1 Cor.
4:10), in order that the wisdom of God might be magnified.
Similarly, he did not rely on his strong personality or persuasive speech, but was with them *in weakness* (v. 3), in order
that the power of God might be displayed in and through
him. He came to Corinth with a foolish message feebly
spoken. We must not minimize what the Apostle here writes.
He is not exaggerating. He is describing the actual physical
weakness from which he was suffering during his first visit
to Corinth. He was afraid. Indeed, he was so nervous as to
be trembling with fear. But he did not resent these humiliating
symptoms. Far from it. He came to see that since human
weakness was a necessary condition of receiving divine power,
God often keeps His servants physically frail. 'We have this
treasure in earthen vessels, to show that the transcendent
power belongs to God and not to us' (2 Cor. 4:7). Tradi-
tion says that Paul was small and ugly. Scripture adds that
he was handicapped by 'a thorn . . . in the flesh', which, what-

ever its exact nature, was almost certainly a physical infirmity, whether persecution or sickness. At first he prayed earnestly to be delivered from it, but Christ revealed to him that His grace was adequate for him, adding, 'my power is made perfect in weakness'. Once persuaded of this, the Apostle could say: 'I will all the more gladly boast of my weaknesses, that the power of Christ may rest upon me', and again 'for when I am weak, then I am strong' (2 Cor. 12:7-10).

I cannot help wondering if this may not be why there are so few preachers whom God is using today. There are plenty of popular preachers, but not many powerful ones, who preach in the power of the Spirit. Is it because the cost of such preaching is too great? It seems that the only preaching God honours, through which His wisdom and power are expressed, is the preaching of a man who is willing in himself to be both a weakling and a fool. God not only chooses weak and foolish people to save, but weak and foolish preachers through whom to save them, or at least preachers who are content to be weak and seem foolish in the eyes of the world. We are not always willing to pay this price. We are constantly tempted to covet a reputation as men of learning or men of influence; to seek honour in academic circles and compromise our old-fashioned message in order to do so; and to cultivate personal charm or forcefulness so as to sway the people committed to our care.

In order resolutely to resist these temptations we shall need strong inducements. It is here that the preacher's basic motives are revealed. If at heart our ambition is self-glorification, we shall continue to use our own power to preach our own wisdom. But if we are deeply concerned for the good of men and the glory of God, we shall not hesitate to sacrifice to these our reputation for wisdom and power.

This was the Apostle Paul's position. He tells the Corinthians that he has deliberately eschewed worldly wisdom and the strength of his own oratory, *that your faith might not rest in the wisdom of men but in the power of God* (v. 15). It had been a tendency of the Corinthians to put their faith in their human leaders (1 Cor. 1:12-15), but Paul would not countenance it. He could not endure the thought that they should repose their confidence in him. He was no fit object for their faith. If they were to put their trust in his wisdom and power, they would be building their house on shifting sand; there is no foundation of rock on which men may safely build but God alone. So for the spiritual good of the Corinthians themselves Paul renounced both lofty words and human wisdom. What was his reputation in comparison with their eternal welfare? He would gladly humble himself for their sake, preaching the foolish message of Christ crucified in power not his own, in order that they might find their salvation in the all-wise, all-powerful God.

The Apostle's second and greater motive, for which he set aside his own wisdom and power, was the glory of God. The consuming passion of his life, to borrow some words of St. Peter, was 'that in everything God may be glorified through Jesus Christ' (1 Pet. 4:11). He was therefore wounded in spirit by the boasting of these Corinthians. He keeps referring to it. Boasting is one of his recurrent themes. '*Le mot l'obsède*', commented Renan. Paul uses it eight times in this epistle and four times in these early chapters. The Corinthians were boasting of themselves and boasting of their human leaders. But the Apostle will have nothing to do with such boasting himself. 'Let no one boast of men', he writes (1 Cor. 3:21). Men have nothing to boast about, since all they possess has been given them. 'If then you received it', he argues, 'why do you boast as if it were not a gift?' (1 Cor. 4:7). No man can save himself and no man can save another man. God is the only Saviour. And God deliberately chooses the weak and foolish 'so that no human being might boast in the presence of God' (1 Cor. 1:29). For the same reason Paul was willing to be a fool and a weakling, in order that: 'Let him who boasts, boast of the Lord' (1 Cor. 1:31). He had no wish to usurp the glory of the Lord. Power for salvation is not in men, whether preachers or hearers; it is in God alone, in the Father's Word, in the Son's death and in the Holy Spirit's witness. So let preacher and congregation humble themselves, willing to be despised as both weak and foolish, in order that all the wisdom and the power of salvation may be ascribed where they belong, namely to the three glorious Persons of the Eternal Trinity.

We come back at last to the phrase with which we began. What are Christian preachers? Paul asks. They are just 'servants through whom you believed, as the Lord assigned to each' — that is, agents through whom God has worked to elicit your faith. This being the case, the glory is not due to the agent through whom the work is done, but to the Lord who does the work by His own power.

I conclude with some words found in the vestries of St. Mary-at-Quay Ipswich, and Hatherleigh Parish Church, and given to me by the Rev. Basil Gough of Oxford:

> *When telling Thy salvation free*
> *Let all-absorbing thoughts of Thee*
> *My heart and soul engross:*
> *And when all hearts are bowed and stirred*
> *Beneath the influence of Thy word,*
> *Hide me behind Thy cross.*